You Shall Be My Witnesses

How to Reach Your City for Christ

LARRY ROSENBAUM

SOS MINISTRIES PRESS
P.O. Box 27054
San Francisco, CA 94127

YOU SHALL BE MY WITNESSES:
HOW TO REACH YOUR CITY FOR CHRIST

Library of Congress Catalog Card Number 86-090426
ISBN 0-938573-00-4

CONTENTS

FOREWORD

THERE WILL BE A TIME
WHEN WE WON'T NEED THIS BOOK . . .

. . . Jesus will be ruling in His Glory, Satan will be expelled, and we will not have to concern ourselves with the present realities of spiritual warfare, nor struggle with the powers of darkness anymore. What a time that will be!

But today we do have to concern ourselves with these matters. The world *is* fallen, people *are* without God, and you and I *are* called to "shout the name of Jesus to a dying world."

Larry Rosenbaum is one of the faithful who has been declaring this name for years, and I know, will continue to do so until he either leaves his body to go be with Jesus, or Jesus comes back. Larry is a leader in the areas of street ministry, evangelism, and spiritual warfare, who is well qualified to write this book, not only from the standpoint of knowing the right things to say, but from the much greater platform of having been a "doer" of these words for many years.

This is a "how-to" book, dispensing practical information in an interesting and digestible way, but it is much more than that at the same time. It is a challenging, inspiring book which will be the seed of many new ministries springing up as a result of the inspiration brought to those who read it. Filled with wisdom and insight, it will enrich you, and challenge your present brand of Christianity. It is my prayer that all who read this book will be moved to *action,* to unite with other members of God's emerging army to do "greater works" than even Jesus did.

This book is the bottom line . . . All our teaching, all our preaching, all our newly acquired revelation knowledge in the

1

areas of faith, prosperity, healing, unity, signs and wonders, worship and warfare are just the preliminaries, the preparation for the main event, the mobilizing of the army of God in the end times to shout the message of Jesus from the rooftops. Larry has written a manual for that army, which will facilitate and greatly enhance our effectiveness as we come against the powers of darkness in earnest to take back some of the devil's territory, and speak the words that will set the captives free.

I count it a privilege to call Larry my friend, and to have been invited to write this foreword, and trust that the seed sown by this book will result in a great multiplication of a so vitally needed brand of ministry.

Read this book and then *GO FOR IT!*

Chuck Girard

PREFACE

Over the past thirty years we have seen our nation (and many nations around the world) turn away from God and Christian morality at a remarkable rate. Our young people are being taught in schools and by parents that there is no God, all morality is relative, and our existence is an accident with no real purpose. Increasing numbers of these children are growing up in broken homes, or foster homes, as their parents get divorced. The "heroes" of millions of our youth are the rock stars, whose songs promote a lifestyle of "sex, drugs, and rock and roll" — plus satanism and occult activity. As a result, increasing numbers of young (and old) people are getting involved in drugs, crime, cults and the occult, homosexuality and other sexual perversions, getting venereal diseases and AIDS, committing suicide, having abortions, and so on.

While these things are more evident in large cities like San Francisco, the effects of this "satanic revival" can be felt in every city and town in America. In recent years, many Christians have been getting involved in political activities, hoping to reverse the trend toward greater immorality. While such activity is needed, the only real solution is for people to experience the life-changing power of Jesus Christ.

All too often, we assume that everyone in America has already heard the gospel. After all, there are lots of churches around for people to attend. Besides, there are hundreds of Christian radio and TV shows. However, many unbelievers never attend an evangelical church, listen to Christian radio or watch Christian TV. Millions of unbelievers are confused by the various "gospels" they have heard, the coldness and apparent hypocrisy they see in many churches, the constant appeals for money they hear on some Christian radio and TV programs.

They need a person to reach out to them with the love of Jesus Christ, to explain the plan of salvation to them clearly and help answer some of their questions, and to show them what Jesus has done in his or her life.

Jesus said, "The harvest truly is great, but the laborers are few. Pray therefore to the Lord of the harvest that he would send forth laborers into his harvest" (Luke 10:2). I believe that God wants to use *you* as a laborer, and to recruit other workers. This book is written to help you do this.

(Note: Scripture quotations are modified from the King James Version. Often, I have changed the wording of scriptures to modernize them and clarify their meaning, after comparing several translations. Also, while I discuss legal issues related to evangelism in several places, I am not a lawyer. Don't rely on my comments regarding any important legal issue. Discuss the matter with an attorney.)

1 ———————————

From Graveyard to Harvest Field

For many years San Francisco has earned a reputation as the graveyard of Christian ministries. Dozens of ministries have come to San Francisco, gotten discouraged by the hardness of people's hearts and lack of results, and left. Almost all of the best-known evangelists have avoided this city.

In the 11 years I have lived in San Francisco, I have seen a tremendous change in this city. God is raising up an army of Christians who are not ashamed to proclaim His Word. Churches from various denominations are beginning to work together in unity to reach people with God's Word.

In the past three months alone —

1. The Full Gospel Business Men's Fellowship had their first airlift to a U.S. city in San Francisco. Several hundred Christian businessmen came to San Francisco for a week-long outreach to this city. They treated hundreds of unsaved businessmen and street people to $12.50 a plate meals at two luncheons at which they gave testimonies of how God had saved them.

2. Evangelist Mario Murillo held a three-day crusade at Davies Hall, home of the San Francisco Symphony. This was the first Christian meeting ever held in this auditorium. Three thousand people attended the final day and many were saved.

3. The San Francisco Foursquare Church held twenty outdoor evangelistic concerts in downtown San Francisco.

4. One hundred people attended an evangelism seminar at San Francisco Christian Center, which began a new street outreach on Friday nights.

5. Over three hundred people came forward to receive free New Testaments at an outreach sponsored by SOS Ministries.

6. Several churches which had experienced declines for years were reporting growth. One church was adding a 1000 seat auditorium to its facilities. For San Francisco, this is a major step as no evangelical church presently has an attendance of 1000. Also, several new churches were growing rapidly.

7. World Challenge, founded by David Wilkerson, made plans for a large summer outreach. David's son, Gary, will be coming to San Francisco to establish a new outreach church.

8. Evangelist Jerry Brandt obtained a 300 foot ship to use for training evangelistic workers for San Francisco, ministry to the poor, and discipling new believers. He began planning weekend evangelism seminars to train hundreds of Christians in street witnessing.

Over the past seven years, thousands of Christians have been recruited to pray for and witness in San Francisco. In part, these changes are the result of their prayers and witnessing. Many Christians ask if street ministry is effective. Only in heaven will we know all the results of our witnessing. But in the remainder of this chapter I want to give some examples of people who were saved on the streets of San Francisco. The names used below are not their real names.

Seven Testimonies

1. After graduating from college, Jim came to San Francisco in the summer of 1980 to study photography at the San Francisco Art Institute. One day, while he was sitting in a bar at the Hilton Hotel, he noticed a gospel tract stuck inside the menu, and began to read it. He called the number on the back, and told the woman who answered that he was a photographer. (This was the first day of our week-long summer outreach.) The woman told him we really needed a photographer and gave him the address of the church we were meeting in.

That night Jim went out on the streets with a team of Christians to photograph the outreach. He was tremendously impressed by the love and excitement he saw in the believers. That night he prayed to receive Christ and was dramatically converted. A week later he began a friendship with a woman who had come to the outreach to witness. They got married a few months later. The next summer, they went to Taiwan as missionaries and school teachers. They stayed there three years and presently are ministering in Israel. I just got a letter from Jim in which he related how God has been using him to reach many people who had never before heard the gospel.

2. Some Christians in the Tenderloin (skid row) district offered a tract to a prostitute named Judy. She cursed at them and refused to take it. However, she was so convicted that a week later she left San Francisco, went to San Jose, committed her life to Christ, and joined Youth With a Mission. One of our workers met her at a Christian conference in Los Angeles. Otherwise we would never have known what had happened.

3. Bill was an alcoholic in the Tenderloin district. One of our videotapes shows him staggering by a group of Christians witnessing in that area. Shortly after that tape was made, Bill got saved and entered Teen Challenge. Bill has finished their program and is now attending Bible College.

4. Steve had a sex-change operation. After living as a woman for several years, he decided he was attracted to women and became a ''lesbian.'' One day, I witnessed to him and his girl friend, thinking I was talking with two lesbians. Six months later, Steve called to tell me he was saved. He went back to living as a man and has remained steadfast in his commitment to Christ for several years.

5. Tony was involved in Satan worship, drugs and homosexuality. Last summer, he surrendered to Christ at one of our outdoor concerts. He moved into our discipleship house and has grown steadily in Christ.

6. I first witnessed to John when he was fourteen. He had just run away from home. He spent the next six years on the streets as a male prostitute. Several Christians witnessed to him during that time. Today he is in Victory Outreach serving Christ.

7. Linda was a cocktail waitress who had been heavily involved in ''new age'' philosophy. Some Christians witnessed to her on the streets last summer and she received Christ. She joined us

for several meetings and was baptized, but soon went back to her old ways. A month ago God spoke to her to quit her job and follow Him. She contacted us and we found a Christian family to take her in and disciple her.

These are a few of many examples I could give. Street ministry *is* effective. God's Word does not return void, and if we sow bountifully we will reap a great harvest. Street ministry is also good for us. Christians who are involved in outreach are likely to be excited about Christ and healthy spiritually. Christians who aren't involved in outreach are usually caught up in their own problems.

There may be a street outreach in your community. If so, I encourage you to get involved in it. If not, God can use *you* to help start an outreach in your area. It's really not that difficult. You don't need to be especially gifted. All you need is to know God and be filled with His Spirit. Throughout history, God has used ordinary people to do his work. Jesus' apostles included several fishermen and a tax collector. Yet they turned their world "upside down." Your community, too, can be transformed by the power of God's Word. God wants to use *you* to reach many people in your city for Jesus.

2

Where do I start?

Witnessing is easy. Jesus said, "You shall receive power, after the Holy Spirit comes upon you, and you shall be my witnesses" (Acts 1:8). Peter, acting on his own strength, denied Christ three times. After he was filled with the Holy Spirit, Peter preached God's Word with boldness and thousands were saved. When he was threatened with prison, Peter proclaimed, "We ought to obey God rather than men."

Peter didn't take any evangelism classes, nor did the others in the early church who "turned the world upside down" (actually rightside up). When they were persecuted, they grew even stronger in their faith, and many were persuaded to trust in Christ by their witness.

Satan found that persecuting the church only made it stronger, but he found a better tool for silencing Christians — complacency. In Revelation 3, Jesus told the church in Laodicea, "Because you are lukewarm and neither cold nor hot, I will spit you out of my mouth. Because you say, I am rich, and increased with goods, and have need of nothing; and you do not know that you are wretched, and miserable, and poor, and blind, and naked." What an apt description of too much of today's church! So many Christians have been lulled to sleep by their prosperity, material comforts, and lack of real persecution. Often, we find ourselves working more than we need to, striving to maintain a lifestyle we don't need. We are left with little time for the things of God. We spend hours in front of the television but have no time for prayer or witnessing.

According to one study, 90% of all Christians today *never* witness to *anyone*. We are afraid — not of real persecution such as being thrown in jail or killed, which almost never happens in America — but of someone thinking that we are a "religious fanatic." Our unsaved friends will accept us as long as we don't try to "push our religion on them" and give them that "fire and brimstone stuff." We don't want to "turn them off to the gospel" so we either don't witness at all or water down God's Word so we don't offend anyone.

Proverbs 29:25 says, "The fear of man brings a snare, but whoever puts his trust in the Lord shall be safe." In order to start witnessing, we need to overcome fear. The only way I know to do this is to step out and start witnessing to someone, trusting the Lord to be with us.

I was saved in a Christian ministry that was very much involved in street evangelism. After I had been a Christian about a month, I went witnessing for the first time. I went with another Christian and let him do all the talking, since I had no idea what to say. I listened as he talked with many different kinds of people, who asked him some difficult questions. I saw that the Holy Spirit gave him wisdom to answer every question.

The second time I went witnessing, I knew that I needed to go up to someone by myself and start a conversation about Christ. I was really scared, but I forced myself to walk up to a stranger. I had decided beforehand to start by asking him, "Do you know Jesus?" I don't remember the exact conversation, but the Holy Spirit gave me the words to share Christ with him. Afterwards, I went up to a second person, still nervous, but this time it was a little easier. By the end of the day, I was much more comfortable witnessing to strangers, confident that God was with me and would use me.

I could have allowed that initial fear to keep me from ever witnessing for the Lord, as many Christians do. But God helped me to overcome that fear, and I believe that He will help any Christian who wants to be used by God to witness to others but is hindered by fear.

You can read every book on witnessing and take every evangelism training course but at some point you need to step out in faith and start witnessing to people. 1 John 4:18 says, "Perfect love casts out fear." It is our love for God and for the lost that motivates us to overcome our fear and start witnessing. Psalm 81:10 says, "Open your mouth wide and I will fill it." As we step out in faith and open our mouth, God will give us the words to share with others. He knows exactly what they need to hear. We don't.

One thing that really helps is to go out with others who are already experienced at witnessing. Are there Christians in your city or town that are involved in street evangelism? If not, call us and we can refer you to a street ministry near you. It is well worth the effort to travel a few hundred miles, if necessary, to get some experience in street witnessing.

One caution: Satan will do everything he can to keep you from witnessing and to get you to stop witnessing once you start. There are two things Satan does not want — for people to get saved and for them to witness to others once they are saved. Satan will give you many excuses not to witness. He will tell you, for example, that you are not called to witness, that you are too busy to witness, or that your witnessing is only turning people off to the gospel. We are in a spiritual war and we should not be ignorant of the enemy's devices.

Finally, I highly recommend that you read *Take Him to the Streets* by Jonathan Gainsbrugh. This book is available from your local Christian bookstore or from Huntington House, Box 53788, Lafayette, LA 70505. It is an extensive manual on street witnessing and has a wealth of valuable information about hundreds of topics related to street witnessing. Some of these topics include: how to write a tract, where to purchase tracts, how to start a conversation, bar witnessing, street preaching, starting a Christian coffeehouse, making a ministry slide presentation, and how to raise funds for your ministry.

Jonathan also publishes an annual *National Street Ministry Directory* — available from Worldshakers for Christ, Box P-1, Felton, CA 95018 — that lists names, addresses, and phone numbers of thousands of street ministries, Christian coffeehouses, and live-in Christian discipleship programs around the country.

Finally, I would encourage anyone interested in street ministry to join the International Street Ministries Association (ISMA). Many street ministries are beginning to join together to share news and help one another become more effective at street witnessing. ISMA publishes a newsletter which contains news of what is happening on the streets around the country and teachings related to street evangelism. It also sponsors street ministry conferences in various parts of the country to provide a way for people interested in street ministry to get to know one another, and to provide teaching on subjects related to street witnessing. If you write me, I can give you information about joining ISMA.

3

Starting a Weekly Street Witnessing Team

Whether you live in a large city or a small town, there are many people around you who need to know Jesus Christ. To reach them, you need to go where they are. In large cities, there are many places to witness. In small towns, it may be harder to find groups of people in one place. Here are some places you can go:

1. Downtown streets.
2. Athletic events. In small towns, sporting events often draw hundreds of people.
3. Parks and beaches.
4. Fairs and parades.
5. Movie theaters. Find out when the show starts or ends.
6. "Cruise strips" where young people drive up and down the street on weekends, while others stand around and watch.
7. High schools. Witness before or after school. If the students leave campus for lunch, witness to them then.
8. Colleges.
9. Video game arcades.
10. Rock concerts.
11. Shopping centers. We'll discuss the laws relating to this in a later chapter.

When Jesus sent his disciples out to witness, he sent them in groups of two or more. You'll want to find one or more Christians to witness with you. The best place to start looking is your church. Do you know someone who might be interested in witnessing with you? Talk to your pastor or youth pastor about the idea. Perhaps your youth group will want to get involved. Call the secretary of your church (or other churches in town) and ask her to put an announcement in their church bulletin or on a bulletin board: "Anyone interested in joining a street witnessing team that is forming, call _____."

You may get a good response and find quite a few people who want to help start a witnessing team. But don't get discouraged if you don't get any immediate response. The idea of witnessing on the streets is still very strange and scary for most Christians. This situation can change, however, with prayer and persistence.

Meeting for Worship and Prayer before Witnessing

Once you have found some Christians who are interested in witnessing (whether 1 or 5 or 20), you need to set aside a regular place and time for your street witnessing team to meet. The time will depend on the schedules of the people involved, and when the people you are trying to reach are on the street. The place can be anywhere — a living room, a room in a church, etc. The important thing is to make sure that the witnessing team goes out every week, whether 1 or 20 people show up. If you can't be there one week, make sure that someone else will be there to lead the team.

Start the meetings on time. Otherwise people will arrive later and later. Spend some time in worship and prayer before going out on the streets. We need to go out in the power of the Holy Spirit, not our own strength. We need to focus our minds on the Lord and seek His guidance and blessing on the time of witnessing. If possible, have someone who can play an instrument lead worship. You can print up songsheets if everyone doesn't know the songs. Worship is not just singing songs. It is a way for us to express our love for God, to acknowledge His greatness, and to thank Him for what He has done for us.

When the children of Israel went to battle, the tribe of

Judah (praise) went first. Many times the children of Israel found deliverance as they praised the Lord. "We wrestle not against flesh and blood, but against principalities, against powers, against the rulers of the darkness of this world, against spiritual wickedness in high places" (Eph. 6:12). "The weapons of our warfare are not carnal, but mighty through God to the pulling down of strongholds" (2 Cor. 10:4). "The god of this world has blinded the minds of them that believe not, lest the light of the glorious gospel of Christ, who is the image of God, should shine unto them" (2 Cor. 4:4).

Satan and his cohorts do not like to hear us praising God. Praise and worship are very effective in scattering demonic forces so that the eyes of unbelievers will be opened to God's Word. As we worship God, we stop thinking about ourselves and our own weaknesses. Instead, we focus our attention on Christ, His power to save, and His love for the lost. This releases our faith to believe that God will work mightily to save people on the streets.

After we have spent some time in God's presence, praising and worshipping Him, the Holy Spirit will lead us into a time of prayer and intercession. The leader can help make this transition by announcing, "Now we are going to have a time of prayer for today's witnessing. I encourage each of you, as the Lord directs, to lead out in a short prayer for the people we will be witnessing to, and that God will guide us and use us today to bring people to Himself. Keep the prayers focused on today's witnessing, not on other things."

After the prayer time, the leader should give some instructions to the group. Explain where you are going, arrange for transportation, and pair people up, having an experienced person go with each inexperienced person, a man with each woman. You may also need to give some basic instructions, answer questions, etc. Arrange a place to meet on the streets before you start witnessing and meet there again at a prearranged time after the witnessing is over. Make sure everyone has tracts, follow-up cards, church invitations, etc. before they leave.

On the Streets

Where should you go? You may want to go to different areas each week or keep going to the same place. Keep your eyes open for special events — sporting events, rock concerts, county fairs, parades. Find out the schedule for a popular movie. There may be a long line outside the theater. Search out new places to witness. Where do people seem to be most responsive to God's Word? Where are people not in a hurry, and most open to talking with someone?

What kind of approach should you use? Usually, our emphasis on the streets is to share with people one-to-one about Christ. Everyone needs to find an approach that he or she is comfortable with. I personally like to begin by offering a person a gospel tract. "Hi. I've got something for you to read today. It's about Jesus Christ . . . What do you think about Jesus?" This immediately lets the person know what I am doing, centers the conversation on Christ, gets the other person involved in the conversation, and lets me find out where they stand with God. Also, the tract stays with the person after we have talked as a reminder of the conversation and a further explanation of the gospel. The tract should be stamped with a local phone number and address where they can learn more about Christ if they want. One caution: a woman should not give out her home address or phone number to men.

Other Christians prefer not to use any literature, but to start a conversation, get to know the person a little, and bring the conversation to Christ. This is more difficult, but can be very effective when you have enough time or will be seeing the person again. One problem, especially in large cities, is that the person may be wondering, "What is this person up to?" In small towns, people are less suspicious of strangers who talk with them.

It is generally best to witness in pairs, with one person doing most of the talking while the partner is praying. The "silent" partner should be ready to share when needed, but should not interrupt. If you go up to two people, each of you can speak with one. If one of the persons is not interested in the gospel, try to keep him busy so he will not distract his friend. Sometimes, you can approach a group of people and start talking with them about Christ. Usually, at least one person will be really interested. You may want to take him aside and talk with him individually.

Occasionally, the group leader and his partner should check out how the other Christians are doing and help with any problems. When the witnessing time is almost over, he may need to remind people that it is time to end their conversations and gather at the prearranged location. If an unsaved person is very receptive to God's Word, the worker can get his name and phone number, and arrange to continue the conversation later. It is a good idea for all the Christians to gather together in one place at the end of the witnessing time to share testimonies, pray for the people they talked with, and thank God for what He has done.

4 ———————————————

The Gospel Message

Making Disciples, not Decisions

Recently, I read a book called *Today's Gospel: Authentic or Synthetic?* (by Walter Chantry, available for $4 from Banner of Truth Trust, Box 621, Carlisle, PA 17013). It compared today's evangelistic methods with the way Jesus dealt with the rich young ruler. This man came to Jesus looking for eternal life. In short, he was just the kind of person we are looking for in our evangelistic endeavors. His only problem was that he needed to recognize that he is a sinner and receive Christ as his Savior. Since he already believed the Bible is God's Word, we would prove to him out of the scriptures that all of us are sinners. We could probably get him to agree to some sin he had committed. Next, we would discuss the need for blood atonement, and how Jesus offered Himself for our sins. Finally, we would invite him to pray to receive Christ as his Savior.

Jesus did something very different. He confronted him with his biggest sin — covetousness — and told him to sell all his possessions and give to the poor, then come and follow Him. The man went away sorrowful. Did Jesus err, making it too difficult for the man to be saved? Was He teaching salvation by works? Couldn't He have urged the man to accept Him as Savior and later on dealt with his sin? The man had only asked for eternal life. He hadn't asked for an abundant, spirit-filled

19

life on earth and treasures in heaven.

The man undoubtedly went away thinking, "I can't give away all my possessions." The disciples were wondering, "Who then can be saved?" Why was Jesus so hard on the rich young ruler? He wanted the man to become deeply convicted of his own sinfulness and his inability to make himself better. Only then could he come to the Lord as the publican did — "God be merciful to me *the* sinner" — and go home truly justified before God.

We do people a great disservice when we cheapen the gospel in order to obtain superficial decisions for Christ. We should not pray with a person for salvation until he is ready. When someone is aware of his sinful condition, that he cannot save himself, and believes that Christ provided for his salvation and is willing to make Christ Lord of his life, then he is ready to receive Christ. We need to encourage him to count the cost.

When someone is ready to receive Christ, it will take little or no persuasion on your part to get him to pray. If he isn't ready and you persuade him to repeat a "sinner's prayer," he won't be born again and you'll only confuse him. When someone tries to witness to him later, he may say, "I tried that before and it didn't work" or "I'm already saved." It is far better to send someone away knowing he is unsaved than thinking he is saved when he isn't. Present God's Word, allow the Holy Spirit to convict the person of sin, and let Him draw the person to Christ in His time.

Explaining the Gospel

Before a person can understand or appreciate the "good news," he needs to know the bad news — that he is a sinner, that he has disobeyed God's law, and that he is separated from God because of his disobedience (Romans 3:23; 6:23a). Next, we can tell him the good news — that Jesus paid the penalty for our sins by dying on the cross (Romans 5:8) and that He rose from the dead so we could have assurance that God had accepted His sacrifice and we have eternal life in Him (1 Cor. 15:3-4). Third, we are saved by faith in Jesus Christ, not by our works (Eph. 2:8-9; Romans 6:23b; 10:9-10). Finally, let him know that he can benefit from what Jesus did by putting his faith and trust in Jesus Christ, making Him his Savior and Lord (John 1:12; Rev. 3:20). The above scriptures are commonly used in witnessing. I recommend that you memorize them.

A person may have heard the gospel many times but never really understood. You may want to explain about the Old Testament system of sacrifices, how the blood of an innocent animal needed to be shed for a person's sins, and that this system was designed to point to Jesus Christ, the Lamb of God who took away our sins. Or you may want to use an analogy. For example, we are like a person who owes a large debt that we could never repay, yet Jesus has paid the debt for us. Or you could compare it to a person sentenced to life in jail for murder, who is offered a pardon. If that person refuses the pardon, he will have to stay in jail.

We should explain the gospel to people from man's viewpoint and God's viewpoint. From man's viewpoint, we come to Christ to receive the benefits of being a Christian: inner peace, purpose in life, relief from guilt, being set free from destructive habits that are causing us pain (bad temper, alcohol addiction, etc.), eternal life in heaven, fellowship with God. From God's viewpoint, we come to Christ because God loves us and desires fellowship with us. Our disobedience to God separates us from Him and grieves God, who is seeking to draw us into fellowship with Himself.

Explain God's Word simply and clearly, in language the person can understand. Be sensitive to the direction of the Holy Spirit as to what, and how much, to share with each person, and when he is ready to receive Christ. Even if a person is not ready to pray for salvation, you can still pray with the person to ask God to reveal Himself in a greater way to him and draw him to Himself, or to pray for some special need, such as healing. Many people are saved after God answers their prayer for healing or helps them with some problem.

Make sure that people understand what they are doing when they pray to receive Christ. We should urge people to come to Christ, but should not apply undue pressure. A person needs to "count the cost." We need to let people know that there is great joy in living for Christ, but there will also be times of difficulty. Friends may make fun of us or reject us. God will want to make changes in certain areas of our lives. We need to be willing to obey Him, knowing that He loves us and "all things work together for good to them that love God" (Romans 8:28). If you concentrate on making disciples (genuine conversions) instead of quick decisions, you will find that follow-up will be much easier and you will see more lasting fruit from your labors.

Follow-up

If you pray with someone to receive Christ, it is very important that you get his name, address and phone number so you can follow up on him. If possible, before you leave, arrange a time and place to meet him the next day. Make sure the person has a New Testament. Have him start reading one of the gospels. Encourage him to share with at least one person about the decision he made and to attend a Bible-believing church. If possible, invite him to come to your church and offer him a ride if he needs one.

The follow-up visit can be at his house, a church, a restaurant, etc. If possible, bring another Christian with you. A man following up on a woman should always bring a woman with him, and vice versa. On the first follow-up visit, you will want to go over the plan of salvation, explain what happens when a person receives Christ, and share briefly about the importance of praying, reading God's Word, fellowshipping with other Christians, and witnessing to others about Christ. The Navigators, Billy Graham, and other ministries have good follow-up materials you can use. Make a friend of the new believer. Find out what his needs and interests are. Invite him over for dinner. Introduce him to other Christians. Let the person know that you really care about him as an individual, not just "another soul saved," a "notch in your Bible."

We who are in evangelistic ministry are under tremendous pressure to produce statistics and examples of people who have been saved through our ministry. We feel that we need to prove to other Christians that our ministry is effective so that they will want to get involved in street ministry and support us financially. People constantly ask me how many people were saved at our last outreach. There are numerous "evangelistic" methods based on sales techniques that will lead to large numbers of "converts." In reality, our persuasive abilities cannot save anyone. If we are not seeing many people saved from our evangelism, we need to pray more fervently that God would move in people's hearts and draw them to Himself, and that He would increase the anointing upon our witnessing, confirming it with signs following. At the same time, we must trust God with the results of our evangelism. It is our job to obey Him in witnessing to others; it is His job to save them. Only in heaven will we see all the fruit of our labor.

5

High-Visibility Evangelism
Part I

One of the biggest problems we have faced in San Francisco is getting people's attention. In this city, there are voices crying out loudly for so many different causes — political causes, Eastern religions, cults, gay rights, etc. The born-again Christians in this city are, for the most part, silent. It is possible to live in this city and almost never hear anything about Christ. While there are lots of church buildings around, a person might have a hard time finding one that is spiritually alive and does not compromise God's Word.

If you can get someone's attention — if he will at least think about Jesus Christ for a few minutes — the Holy Spirit can use this to convict the person of his sin and need of salvation. In this chapter (and the next), I want to share briefly about some of the methods we have used to get people's attention — what I call "High-Visibility Evangelism."

Open Air Preaching

Open air preaching, of course, is not a new method. We find it throughout the Bible. The Old Testament prophets were essentially street preachers. Noah was called a "preacher of righteousness" as he built an ark, warning the people of God's impending judgment. Noah is quite an encouragement to me when I don't see a lot of results from my witnessing. Noah preached God's Word for up to six hundred years and only his family was saved, yet he was perfectly in God's will. Then there was Jonah, who went to the Gentile city of Ninevah, warning them of God's judgment. Jonah had no love for the people he was preaching to, yet the entire city of over 120,000 repented and escaped destruction. Many of the prophets were imprisoned and put to death because their message was unpopular. God told some of the prophets to do some outrageous things to dramatize His Word, such as walking around naked for three years (Isa. 20), and cooking with excrement (Ezek. 4). I'm sure glad we're living in New Testament times!

Much of Jesus' ministry was that of a street preacher, as He went from town to town preaching God's Word in public places. He sent out the 12 and later the 70 disciples to do likewise. Before He ascended to heaven, He told His disciples, ''Go into all the world and preach the gospel to all creation'' (Mark 16:15).

The book of Acts begins with the words of Jesus, ''You shall receive power after the Holy Spirit has come upon you and you shall be witnesses unto me . . . unto the uttermost part of the earth.'' The rest of the book relates how Peter, Paul, and the other disciples preached God's Word boldly in public places. They were persecuted, but this did not stop them. After Stephen was killed, ''Saul made havoc of the church, entering into every house, and dragging off men and women, putting them in prison. Therefore they that were scattered abroad went everywhere preaching the Word'' (Acts 8:3,4). It wasn't just a few leaders who did the preaching, but the entire church. This is one of the reasons that the early church turned the world ''upside down.'' They weren't paying a few pastors and evangelists to hold meetings inside some buildings, but they were all preaching boldly wherever they went. How we need to do this today!

Considering how much importance is placed on open air preaching in the Bible, it is truly amazing how little of it is done by ''Bible-believing'' churches today. In most cities and towns in America today, few if any people are preaching in public places!

I witnessed on the streets for about seven years before I began street preaching. When I came to San Francisco, I saw a number of street preachers who would preach at Market and Powell, near the cable car turnaround. Many of them spent a lot of time arguing with one another, calling one another "devils" because they disagreed on some doctrine. Many of these street preachers did not have any regular church involvement. What I saw definitely did not make me want to be a street preacher.

After a few years, I met some other street preachers who joined us for our outreaches. They were good, solid Christians who preached under the direction of the Holy Spirit. Sometimes the message was strong, emphasizing the holiness of God. At other times it was very gentle, emphasizing God's love. Several of these preachers encouraged me to start preaching.

I resisted for two reasons: 1) My voice isn't very loud and 2) I was afraid my mind would go blank while I was preaching. One of the preachers loaned me his megaphone, which took care of my first excuse. The Holy Spirit reminded me how He had always given me words to witness to individuals, and assured me that if I would open my mouth to preach, He would give me the words to speak.

My first street preaching experience was much like my first witnessing experience. I was very nervous but the Lord helped me through it. The next time was a little easier, and now it is not difficult to preach to groups of people. One thing I found is that God has given me a unique style of preaching, and He has me preach in different ways to different groups. I have met many anointed street preachers, each of whom has his own God-given style.

After you have been witnessing for a while, I would encourage you to start preaching. Get a megaphone if necessary. (*Take Him to the Streets* has information about where to get one.) Pray, asking the Lord to give you a message and boldness to preach the message under His anointing. He may give you some scriptures to read. Then — open your mouth and He will fill it.

"For Christ sent me . . . to preach the gospel: not with

wisdom of words, lest the cross of Christ should be made of no effect . . . . For after that in the wisdom of God the world by wisdom knew not God, it pleased God by the foolishness of preaching to save them that believe. For the Jews require a sign, and the Greeks seek after wisdom: But we preach Christ crucified, unto the Jews a stumbling block, and unto the Greeks foolishness'' (1 Cor. 1:17-23).

We need to understand these verses. Our preaching will look foolish and be rejected by a lot of people. But it is God's plan to save those who in simple childlike faith will believe the message of the cross. I don't want to turn people off by a sloppy appearance or by unkind remarks, but I can expect that some people will be turned off by our preaching. In Galatians 5:11, Paul talks about the ''offense of the cross.'' The only way to avoid offending people is by not preaching the gospel. Unfortunately this is what most Christians do.

If you are obedient to Christ's command to preach His Word, you can be assured that God's Word will not return void, but will accomplish the purpose God has intended for it (Isa.55:11). After Stephen was killed, Saul went out to see how many Christians he could throw in jail. But when Jesus appeared to him later, He said, ''It is hard for you to kick against the pricks'' (Acts 9:5). Saul's conscience had been bothering him. God had used the preaching of Stephen, as well as the witness of other Christians, in Saul's life.

In large cities, there are many good places to preach, where a lot of people will hear the message. But even in smaller cities and towns there are good places to preach: on Main Street, at the high school, at a rock concert, parade, or county fair, outside the movie theater, or at a college campus. Street preaching in a small town can be very effective. People have probably never seen this before in their town. You'll become the talk of the town and may get front page coverage in the local paper! People may make fun of you, but it will show them that you're serious enough about what you believe to risk the disapproval of others. It just might cause them to take God's Word seriously.

Satan knows the power of gospel preaching, so he will do anything he can to discourage you from preaching on a consistent basis. You will be attacked, but remember where these attacks are coming from. Satan will even use misguided Christians. They will tell you that you are turning people off, hurting the cause of Christ, and what you are doing is definitely not of God. When you hear these things you need to respond in love, to pray for them, and check your own heart to make sure you are preaching with an attitude of genuine love for the lost. It is easy to allow our own personal frustrations to enter into our preaching, to get angry at people because they don't seem to be responding. If we preach a strong message, we need to be certain that it is coming from God, not from our flesh. At the same time, do not allow yourself to fall into condemnation, and don't listen to Satan's lies.

6 —————————————

High-Visibility Evangelism Part II

Tract Distribution

Often, when I am out on the streets, I will find myself mainly giving out tracts to people. In some places, like the business district, people are in a hurry and won't stop to talk, but most will take a tract. The same is true at crowds leaving athletic events or rock concerts, at parades or other events. In large cities, people are less likely to get into a conversation with a stranger, but most people do take tracts.

There are many advantages to using tracts. A well-written tract has a clear explanation of the plan of salvation and a prayer the person can use to receive Christ. It also has an address and phone number for the person to call if he wants more information. We constantly get calls and letters from our tracts, having distributed several million. Some people have questions or need help. Others have received Christ from the tract. Many people tell me they collect tracts and read them from time to time. Often a person will read a tract when he is depressed or in a crisis. If a person is drunk, or doesn't want to talk to you while his friends are around, he can take the tract home and read it later in the privacy of his home. Even if he throws the tract on the ground, tears it up, or throws it in the trash can, someone else may pick it up, read the tract or fragment of the tract, and get saved! I know of several instances where this has happened. If someone doesn't speak English, you can give him a tract in his language (preferably with the address and phone number on it of a local church where his language is spoken).

You can probably find some good tracts at your Christian bookstore. There are tract companies that will send out tracts for free, or on a donation basis. Write us, and we can send you some addresses. Or you can write and print up your own tracts. You can either use general-purpose tracts or tracts for special events, such as a Fourth of July parade or Christmas. We write most of the tracts we use, and print them inexpensively. We try to relate our tracts to the things people in San Francisco are interested in, and to write them in a contemporary style.

Giving out tracts is one of the easiest things you can do, but more people will take them if you follow a few guidelines. Dress neatly, smile, and be assertive. The busier people are, the more aggressive you need to be. Stand directly in front of someone and say in a loud voice: "Hi. Here's something for you to read," or "Did you get one?" If people aren't in such a hurry, you might add, "It's about Jesus" and sometimes they will stop and talk. This is a good way to filter out those who are receptive in a large crowd. Sometimes, if you say it's about Jesus the person will refuse it, whereas if you don't say anything they'll at least read part or perhaps all of the tract. If you hold out the tract near their hand, they are more likely to take it. If you act like what you're giving out is good news and important, which it is, people are more likely to receive one. If you look dejected, people probably won't want to read what you're giving out. These are simple suggestions, but they make a big difference.

I try to carry tracts with me wherever I go. You can give out tracts to people you pass on the street, to the person sitting next to you on the bus or to everyone on the bus. You can leave tracts in all sorts of places, such as in phone booths or with a tip in a restaurant.

Carry special tracts for children as well as adult tracts. Children from 7-11 years old usually cannot understand adult tracts. However, they are normally very receptive to God's Word and will read carefully a tract designed for them. Almost all children will take a tract they are offered, unless their parents have instructed them not to take anything from a stranger.

Using Signs and Banners, Carrying a Cross, Marches

Signs are an extremely easy and effective method of witnessing, yet Christians almost never use them. Political protest groups and labor unions know the power of signs, and have used them for years. A dozen people carrying signs looks like a major event. If the event is put on TV, it can influence millions of people.

People read signs. Someone may refuse to talk with you, may refuse a tract, but they *will* read the sign you're carrying that gives a brief portion of the gospel message, and they'll think about it. Signs are about the only way to witness to all the people who are driving by while you're out on the streets. Many bars and restaurants have large windows. The people inside will read your sign as you walk by. Signs attract people's attention. Often, they'll come up to you and ask you why you're carrying the sign or what you're protesting. This gives you a perfect opportunity to witness.

It is easy to make a sign using stencils, poster paint or magic markers, cardboard, a stick and nails. The message you use on a sign needs to be brief. Some of the messages we have used include:

1. Open your heart to Jesus.
2. Ask me about Jesus.
3. One way to God: Jesus.
4. Wise men still seek Him.
5. To know Jesus is to love Him.
6. I love Jesus.
7. Where will you spend eternity?
8. Jesus is alive!
9. What will you say on judgment day?
10. Jesus Christ: our only hope.
11. Jesus Christ is God.

We have a large blue nylon banner that reads "Jesus Christ

is Lord" on one side and "Jesus Saves Sinners" on the other — in 20 inch letters. Whenever we have concerts we put up this banner in the most conspicuous place and thousands of people read it. Recently we've started taking the banner witnessing with us. When we are witnessing on a crowded street, we tie up the banner between two poles. We do the same thing at rock concerts. We put up the banner so everyone can read it as they leave the concert.

In recent years, Arthur Blessitt popularized the idea of carrying a cross down the street, witnessing to people about Jesus. Everyone knows what the cross represents. As you carry it, people are reminded of what Jesus did for them. Often, they will ask you why you are carrying the cross. Some people make large crosses with a wheel on the bottom. One person I know uses a styrofoam cross! When we carry a cross down a street known for wickedness, people really come under conviction as they think about what Jesus did for them, and how they are not following the Lord.

You can combine these methods by having a march for Jesus. We do this a lot and find it very effective at getting people to think about Jesus. Take a group of Christians — 10, 100, 1000, or more and start marching down the street. If possible, bring a cross, lots of signs and banners, and some guitars and other instruments. Sing worship songs as you march.

Each summer we have a week-long outreach called "SOS-San Francisco." On the last day of the outreach, we march through downtown San Francisco with hundreds of Christians. We end the march at the fountain in front of City Hall, where we baptize the new believers who were saved during the outreach. This is a powerful witness to the unsaved and a great encouragement to the Christians.

Street Music and Drama

People really like to be entertained. An individual or group singing songs or doing a drama skit portraying some aspect of God's Word will draw a crowd. A group of Christians can practice some songs with a guitar, or learn a short skit in a few hours. A professional-quality group can gather hundreds of people and hold their attention for an hour or more. You may not do as well, but you will draw some people with a few songs or a short skit. A good book on street drama is *Harvesting the Field* by Kirk Henneberry, 401 N College, Decatur, IL 62522.

Church on the Street

Many people refuse to step inside a church building, except for a wedding or funeral. Some claim that they had a bad experience in a church or are turned off by the coldness and hypocrisy they saw. Others think themselves unworthy to enter a church building. If people will not come into a church building, we can — and should — bring the church to them.

The church, of course, is not a building but the body of believers God has called out of the world unto Himself. The early Christians did not have special church buildings. They met in homes and in public places such as Solomon's porch on the Temple grounds (Acts 5:12). When we have church services in public places, it gives unbelievers an opportunity to experience the presence of the Holy Spirit, the beauty of worship, the love, joy, and peace that is felt as believers gather together, and the reality of knowing Christ. Demonic powers are scattered when Christians gather in true worship, and an atmosphere is established in which unbelievers are convicted of their sin and drawn to Christ.

There are several ways to adapt a church service to a street situation. One is for a church to hold its regular worship service in a public park. An alternative is to have a special worship service at a different time, such as Sunday afternoon after church or Saturday afternoon. Talk to your pastor about this idea. If you pick a busy park and meet there on a regular basis, such as the first Sunday of each month, people will start joining you and some will get saved and be added to your church.

Outdoor church services are also a good, non-threatening way of getting people in your church involved in witnessing. If you use a public address system, people will hear you better. This may require renting a generator and a small P.A. (public address) system, if you don't have one. Call the police department to find out if a permit is needed and, if so, how to get one.

The service needs to be adapted to meet the needs of unbelievers. A few brief testimonies of salvation and of God's workings in the lives of believers are helpful. Avoid using Christian jargon such as "sanctified" and "propitiation" without explaining the terms. After the message, give people an opportunity to receive Christ or receive prayer for personal needs. Keep the meeting short. We have a policy of not taking offerings in evangelistic gatherings, since it confirms the suspicions of many unbelievers that we are only "after people's money." After the meeting you can serve refreshments, giving the Christians an opportunity to meet the new people and speak with them informally.

Another thing you can do is organize a special worship rally in a local park. Several times a year we gather hundreds of Christians from different local churches for a worship rally in a downtown park on Saturday afternoon. We get a permit (ask your police department how to get one), set up a large public address system, and have a worship group lead in worship for an hour. This is followed by a 20 minute evangelistic message and an opportunity for people to come forward to receive salvation, prayer for personal needs, or to get a free New Testament. During the worship time, the presence of the Holy Spirit is very strong and hundreds of unbelievers are drawn to listen. Some of the Christians are trained to counsel and pray with those who come forward. Other Christians are looking around for unbelievers who are being touched by God's Spirit, and get into conversations with them about Christ. Still others are standing around the periphery of the park, giving out tracts and inviting people to join the rally.

A third method we have used with great success in San Francisco is called "church on the street." Our regular street witnessing team will gather on a busy sidewalk, making sure to leave a pathway for people to walk by so we don't block the sidewalk. Usually, we start with a few worship songs, have a one minute testimony, worship for 5 more minutes, and have someone preach for 2 minutes, closing with an invitation for people to come forward and receive Christ.

Often, when our street witnessing team first gathers on a street, the whole team will worship on the street for about 15 minutes. Then, we will send most of the Christians in pairs to witness and leave about 10 Christians at that spot to continue in worship. Occasionally, someone will preach a short message. This helps establish an atmosphere where the presence of God is felt, in contrast to the other things that are happening on the street. Workers who get spiritually drained while out on the street can join the worship group for a while and get refreshed.

Balloons, Stickers, Posters, Floats

We should constantly be looking for new ways of getting God's message to people. One method that has been used effectively is giving away helium balloons with something about Christ printed on it. People will stand in line to get a balloon, and carry it around the city with God's Word on it. Balloons are especially effective at special events such as parades. Ed Human is an evangelist who has used balloons for years. You can order balloons from him, as well as get information about how to use them. His address is Box 1403, Euless, TX 76039. Ed also prints stickers with a Christian message. You can put them all sorts of places. Also, you can give them away to people on the street.

Before he was saved, Ron Woodruff received some Jesus stickers at the Mardi Gras in New Orleans. He couldn't read but he liked the fluorescent stickers and put them up in his room. His friends would come into his room, read the stickers, and ask him if he believed in God. God used this to get him thinking about Jesus.

Another thing you can do is put tracts or specially-designed Christian posters up on bulletin boards and any other place where there are fliers announcing various events. In doing this, we need to avoid defacing property and bringing reproach to Jesus.

One idea that few Christians have considered is putting a Christian float in a parade. All you need to do is get a flatbed truck and decorate it with some Christian theme. Make an attractive float that can be used at any event. Pick a parade at a small town near you and apply to enter. Small parades usually will accept anyone who applies. Being in a parade gives you an opportunity to witness to everyone there. You can set up a sound system on the float and talk about Jesus, or play Christian music. Other Christians can walk along the float and give out tracts. This is an especially good way to give tracts to children. Once you have been in one parade, you will find it easy to get into larger parades. In fact, you will probably receive application forms for parades without asking for them. I have met some Christians who have a ministry of putting a float in parades all over Northern California. This is an easy and effective way of reaching millions of people.

The Effectiveness of High-Visibility Evangelism

In San Francisco, as in many other cities, the voices advocating sexual immorality, drug abuse, occultic activities, and Eastern religions and cults are very loud. The voices calling people to turn from such things to faith in God through Jesus Christ have been virtually silenced. As God's Word is proclaimed boldly and openly in the public places of the city, people will be continually confronted with their need to make a decision regarding Jesus Christ. Satan is seeking to distract people from that reality, and we need to remind people that they have a choice to make which will determine their eternal destiny.

Since so many Christians question the effectiveness of street preaching, tract distribution, carrying signs and other high visibility methods, let me give eight ways in which these methods are effective in advancing God's kingdom on this earth:

1. They help people to learn how they can be saved. Often, people have read dozens of tracts and may even collect them. They may never have prayed to receive Christ, but they know what they need to do and are familiar with many of the scriptures relating to salvation.

2. They cause people to become conscious of God's Word and their need to make a decision either to accept or reject Jesus

Christ. Each time a person is confronted with the gospel, he must think about Christ and his need for salvation. God can use each witness to draw the person closer to Himself.

3. They leave people without excuse. God has given each person a free will — to accept or reject Him. If he chooses to reject the truth, he will give account of his life before God on Judgment Day. He will not be able to say he never heard the gospel, or had no opportunity to be saved.

4. They cause an entire city or nation to become more conscious of God's Word. Often, we find that when we witness at major events, people comment that we are everywhere. People start expecting Christians to witness to them at rock concerts, parades, downtown parks, etc. They start talking with one another about all the Christian activity. They are impressed by the dedication they see in us.

5. The atmosphere of a city or neighborhood can change. Demonic principalities loose their hold on an area where Christ is consistently preached and worshipped. As the Holy Spirit descends upon an area, demonic strongholds are broken up and people become more open to God's Word. Demons cannot stay in a place where Christ's Lordship has been established.

6. The Christians who participate will be strengthened spiritually. We have found that many of those who participate in our outreaches find that they have become bolder in witnessing in other situations. They become more excited about their Lord, as they see Him using them to witness to others. Their desire to intercede for the lost increases, as does their desire to grow spiritually so that their lives will be a better witness for Jesus. Their renewed excitement about the Lord spreads to other Christians.

7. Other Christians are encouraged by our boldness to witness for Christ. After seeing what we are doing, many Christians have been encouraged to witness to their friends, or even to start a street ministry in their own community.

8. Many people do get saved as a result of preaching. However, we only get to see a small percentage of the fruit. Some come to the Lord on the street and we are able to follow-up on them. Others are saved on the street but we lose track of them, or we do not see an immediate change in their lives. In many cases, the person may not get saved until much later. The person who witnessed to him may never learn about it in this life.

7

Getting Your Church Involved in Street Witnessing

When most of us hear the word "evangelist" we immediately think of someone like Billy Graham who holds large crusades and leads lots of people to Christ. While this is one function of the evangelist, he also has another important function. Ephesians 4 says that God gave evangelists "to equip the saints for the work of the ministry, for the building up of the body of Christ."

Not every Christian is an evangelist, but every Christian is called to witness for Jesus. The evangelist is supposed to help train believers to witness for the Lord. When I go out on the streets to witness, only certain people will respond. Some people can't relate to me because I'm too old or too young, they don't like the way I look or talk, or for some other reason. Even though the message is the same, God uses a wide variety of messengers and approaches to reach different people. So we need a lot of workers with a variety of witnessing styles and personalities to reach different people on the streets.

Many people are saved at mass meetings, such as Billy Graham crusades. Others won't go near an evangelistic crusade. Many people are saved by watching Christian television. Others can't stand "TV preachers." Many people are saved by the witness of Christian friends or relatives. Others don't have any Christian friends or relatives, or won't receive their witness. Some people will not talk to strangers. Others will open up to a stranger on the street, but not to their friends or relatives. We need to reach people for Jesus through *every possible means*.

Jesus said, "The harvest is ripe, but the laborers are few." By myself, I can witness to a few people. If I can recruit and train other laborers, I can multiply my ministry. God showed me that He wants to use this book to help train workers to start street ministries in cities and towns throughout this country, and in other countries.

While there are many Christians in the United States, very few are actively witnessing for the Lord. Many people in this country are turning away from God, especially young people, and getting involved in drugs and sexual immorality, among other things. In other countries, the needs are even greater. There are many groups of people throughout the world that have no Christian witness at all. It is my hope that God will use this book to encourage Christians to go into all the world with His Word. Even in the United States, we can witness to people from every nation on the earth. As these people are saved, many will take the gospel to their homelands.

Usually, there are a few people in each church who are eager to witness. Often these are people God has called to be evangelists. God has placed evangelists in each church, not only to witness, but to equip and encourage other believers in the church to witness. Frequently, these evangelistically-oriented Christians are frustrated by the lack of interest in evangelism by others in their church.

How do we get people in our church interested in witnessing? Let me give a few suggestions. *First, pray for the people in your church, especially your pastor*. Ask God to give these people a burden for the lost. Pray that He would send forth laborers into the harvest out of your church. Pray that your pastor would encourage people in your church to get involved in street ministry, and that he would be involved himself. Persevere in prayer. Keep praying that God would move in the lives of people in your church.

Second, try to get the support of your pastor. In the Bible, people are often compared to sheep. They follow their leader. Your pastor may not be an evangelist, but if he believes in the importance of evangelism, if he encourages those in his church to witness, and especially if he sets an example for his flock by participating in street ministry himself, many of the "sheep" will follow. There are a few churches in the San Francisco area in which a large portion of the believers are involved in evangelism. In almost every case, the pastor is very supportive of street witnessing, and joins the group occasionally.

Go to your pastor and tell him about the street ministry you are involved in. Ask his help in getting others in the church involved. He may give you an opportunity to speak about the ministry during a service, or to give testimonies of what has happened on the street from time to time. Also, he will probably allow you to put an announcement in your church bulletin. He may give you an opportunity to teach a class on street witnessing.

People will listen to what your pastor says and does more than they will listen to you. Ask him if he would announce the street witnessing and really encourage people to get involved. Ask him if he would be willing to join you occasionally, perhaps once a month. If he announces the street ministry, says that he believes it is an important ministry, and that he will be there this Saturday (or whenever), you will probably get a good turnout from your church.

Third, get your church involved in follow-up. Find some people in your church who have a burden to follow up on new believers. Give them names, addresses, and phone numbers of people you have met on the streets who have received Christ or shown an interest in Him. As they minister to these people, and as some of the new believers start coming to your church, people will see that street witnessing is an effective ministry and they will start getting a burden for these people, and others like them who need the Lord. As they talk to some confused teenager who comes from a broken home and is addicted to drugs, God will give them love for the many people who are caught up in such lifestyles.

Fourth, be positive. Most Christians know that they should be witnessing more than they do, and already feel guilty about it. Usually, this guilt is not sufficient to motivate them to witness. If you are constantly reminding people of how they should be witnessing more, and of all the people going to hell while they are watching TV, they will avoid you and not listen to what you say. Occasionally, we do need to speak of these things, but mostly we need to relate the exciting things that happened on the streets. Talk about the people who get saved, or respond positively. Let them know how you have grown spiritually from your involvement in street ministry. Avoid talking about persecution and negative responses as it tends to scare people off. When you're actually getting persecuted, God gives you great joy. But those who have never witnessed don't know this.

Fifth, get the new believers in your church out on the streets. They're excited about the Lord and want to tell others about what they've experienced. With a little instruction, they can be very effective witnessers. Often, new believers lead more people to Christ than more mature Christians do. Their Christian experience is fresh and exciting, as ours should be. They are filled with the joy of the Lord and they still remember how to relate to unbelievers. They read about Jesus' command to preach the gospel to every creature and they naturally want to obey. Be sure that they witness with a mature believer, and be careful that they are not drawn back into their old lifestyles. In San Francisco, we have had a real problem with ex-homosexuals witnessing in homosexual neighborhoods. This could also be a problem with ex-alcoholics, ex-pornography addicts, etc.

Finally, don't get discouraged. Few things are more difficult than getting Christians involved in street evangelism. Many people have attended their church for many years without hearing that they should witness on the streets or seeing anyone from their church participate in street evangelism. They may have seen a street preacher who looked like a wild fanatic. They may think that America is already well-evangelized with Christian TV and radio, evangelistic crusades, and churches in every neighborhood. They hear about all the world's problems through TV and newspapers, but it doesn't hit home (unless they learn that their son or daughter is on drugs, or is a homosexual).

It has been said that the last seven words of a dying church are: "We never did it this way before." As Christians, we tend to get set in our ways. But things in your church can change with prayer, persistence, gentle persuasion, and hopefully the support of your pastor.

One of the greatest enemies of the church is our material wealth. When we get comfortable, our prayer life becomes less intense. Society will accept us as long as we don't "rock the boat" by witnessing too much. It may take persecution to stir up the church in America. We need to pray for spiritual revival and do all we can to encourage our brethren to become true disciples of the Lord. We need to set a good example ourselves. We must be on our guard not to get caught up in worldly cares and desires. Be sure to exhort others with love and humility, not self-righteousness.

8 ─────────────────────

Some Places To Witness

1. Shopping Center Evangelism

San Francisco is an ideal city for street witnessing. Any time, day or night, you can find people on the streets to witness to. It never gets very cold here and the rain usually doesn't last too long. However, you may live in a small town where the streets are dead after 6 PM. Winters may be horribly cold. Where can you go to witness? Chances are, there is a shopping center somewhere near you. The problem is that shopping centers have security guards and usually have "no soliciting" rules. How do you get around this?

First, nobody can prevent you from talking with people about Christ, as long as you don't force people to talk with you. If a security guard complains, ask him two questions: 1) Are all conversations about religion prohibited in this shopping center? and 2) Are all conversations with strangers prohibited? The First Amendment to the Constitution clearly prevents any such restriction. If he says that the shopping center prohibits soliciting or loitering, explain to him that soliciting means asking for money (or approaching for an immoral purpose) and loitering means being somewhere with no good purpose. So these do not apply to you.

A shopping center can prevent you from distributing literature, but not from giving out a tract to someone you are talking with. And you can give out literature until an official asks you to stop. By the way, the same is true of stores, restaurants, buses, or any place that is open to the public. You can give out literature until some official tells you to stop.

Second, you can use entertainment as a means to witness. Sometimes shopping centers allow music, drama, clowns, or other entertainment. Perhaps you can get permission from the management to perform. At Christmas and Easter times, religious music is particularly welcome, and often you can share the gospel openly.

Third, you can go to the management and ask permission to set up a table and give out literature about Christ. If they object, inform them of the U.S. Supreme Court decision, Pruneyard Shopping Center vs. Michael Robins, 64 L ED 2d 741, 100 S Ct 2035, decided June 9, 1980. In this case, some students seeking support for a political position set up a table in a shopping center in California and began distributing pamphlets and asking passers-by to sign a petition. A security guard told them they could not do this. The California Supreme Court ruled that the California Constitution gave these students the rights they were exercising, and that they did not infringe on the property rights of the shopping center owners. On appeal, the U.S. Supreme Court agreed.

This means that a shopping center owner in California cannot deny you the right to give out literature or set up a table in their shopping center. In other states, it may be necessary to take the matter to court, but it is likely that the result would be the same. The rights given to citizens under the California Constitution are essentially the same as those in other state constitutions, and in the U.S. Constitution as well.

If you go to the management of a shopping center with a copy of this Supreme Court decision (*we'll send you one free on request*), he may allow you to set up a table and give out literature in his shopping center. If not, you may want to contact a Christian lawyer. The Christian Legal Society, P O Box 2069, Oak Park, IL 60303, can help you find one. Often a letter from a lawyer will be sufficient. Remember that the management does not want the adverse publicity and expense that will come from a lawsuit, especially one they will probably lose.

If the management won't back down, you need to decide whether to go to court. If that shopping center is the best place to witness in your area, it may be wise to go to court. Also, a favorable court decision will help Christians in other places who want to witness in shopping centers. But you need to count the cost. Legal action can take a lot of time, energy, and money. Even if you get free legal help, it's costing the lawyer his time. Nonetheless, there are times when we must fight for our rights, or we will lose them. The apostle Paul took advantage of his rights as a Roman citizen, and several times rebuked officials who acted illegally. One thing that we need to remember is that the shopping center administrator is not our enemy. We must relate to him with kindness and respect, showing him Christ's love.

2. Rock Concert Evangelism

Over the past twenty years, millions of young (and older) people have been influenced toward a lifestyle involving "sex, drugs, and rock and roll." Every city has rock concerts that draw thousands of people. This gives us an excellent opportunity to witness to large groups of people we might not otherwise reach, in a situation where the light of Christ contrasts with the darkness of the world.

In our witnessing at rock concerts, we preach with a megaphone, use signs, give out tracts, and share with people individually. Preaching and signs get people's attention and get them thinking about Christ. Most will take gospel tracts and, while some tracts get thrown on the ground, many get read. Often, before a concert, there are long lines and you can talk with those who are waiting in line. After a concert, you can talk with people who are waiting for a ride or a bus. We have a giant banner that reads "Jesus Christ is Lord" in 20 inch letters. We put it up across the street so everyone can read it as they drive home.

Usually, you can find out about the major rock concerts from your newspaper. If you are going before the concert, you should be there one or two hours before it begins. Usually, you can find out when a concert ends by calling the promoter. Be there about thirty minutes before it ends as the crowd will leave quickly. After the concert, people are more intoxicated, but they are more likely to take a tract home and think about what you said on their way home. Before a concert, people are excited about getting into the concert. Afterwards, they may be disappointed and thinking that there must be a better way to live.

A crowd of intoxicated kids can be intimidating. Some will threaten you with violence. In our experience, these threats have never been carried out. Others will tell you that you are turning kids off to the gospel, or that nobody is interested in what you are saying. Actually, the more effective you are, the more Satan will try to discourage you from witnessing. It has been said that when you throw a stone at a pack of dogs, the one that yells the loudest is the one that got hit. Often, the person who complains the loudest about your preaching is the one who is being most deeply convicted by the Holy Spirit.

At the same time, we need to make sure that we are preaching out of love, and that we stick to the gospel. Some young people think we are preaching that they should stop listening to rock music and start listening to old-time gospel hymns. In my witnessing, I sometimes talk about the lyrics of the songs, and how they often have an anti-Christian message, but I don't criticize people for their musical tastes. We are not preaching that people should stop taking drugs or going to rock concerts, but that they need to make Jesus Christ their Savior and Lord.

Of course, the best way to witness at a rock concert is to get inside and speak to the whole group over the P.A. stytem. Some Christian music groups are able to play at secular concerts and sing about Christ. Also, you can contact a promoter and ask to speak for five minutes at intermission. It doesn't hurt to ask. Some promoters are concerned about their public image, or feel guilty about what they are doing, and may be willing to give you "equal time." You can also try this at smaller clubs. Once I was preaching outside a large punk rock club when the owner invited me to come inside. He let me preach to the crowd over the

P.A. system for about five minutes, and to answer some questions from them about Christ. An alternative for those who are bold is to buy a ticket to the concert, go inside, and ask God to give you an opportunity to walk on stage, pick up the microphone, and start preaching about Jesus. Christians have witnessed to many thousands of people this way.

3. Witnessing at High Schools and Colleges

Most people who receive Christ do so before they are eighteen. Many young people today grow up with little or no knowledge of the gospel. Most schools will not allow you to go on the campus, but you can witness as the students come to school in the morning, during lunch time (if they leave campus), or when the students go home from school. You can find out their schedule by calling the school.

You may run into opposition from school officials or the police to witnessing near a school. They can prohibit you from witnessing on the grounds of a high school, but not from the sidewalk or "public easement" in front of the school. You can find out where the public easement is in front of any building by calling city hall.

Some Christians have been able to speak in high school assemblies and classes about topics such as drug abuse or abortion. While they can't directly preach the gospel, they can bring in their personal testimony and share indirectly about Christ. Some will rent the school auditorium after school for a Christian meeting, and will arrange to speak in the assembly during the day about a topic such as drug abuse or dating. Meanwhile, campus Christians will invite other students to the meeting after school at which the gospel is openly presented.

The best way to reach high school students is through Christians who attend that school. They are free to witness to their friends all they want. Unfortunately, most teenage Christians are too weak in their commitment to Christ and too much influenced by peer pressure to witness effectively to their unsaved friends. However, Christians in high schools who are dedicated to Christ and not ashamed of Him will be used mightily to reach others in their school. Teenagers are looking for direction for their lives and usually are receptive to the gospel, especially if they know Christians who are walking close to the Lord.

College campuses are also good places for evangelism. At most colleges, people will be advancing a variety of religious and political causes on campus. A school may attempt to keep "outside groups" off campus, but their position would probably not hold up in court. Also, if they allow any outside group on campus, they must allow you as well. Normally, you can clear up any problem by talking to the proper school official and explaining what you are doing, and mentioning your First Amendment rights. You may avoid problems by getting a campus ministry to sponsor you.

In witnessing to college students, it is good to have some knowledge of apologetics. "Be ready always to give an answer to every man that asks you a reason for the hope that is in you" (1 Peter 3:15). In my opinion, the best book on the subject is *Evidence that Demands a Verdict* by Josh McDowell, which is available at most Christian bookstores. We need to know that there are intelligent answers to people's questions and we should discuss these things with those who are honestly seeking truth. However, we should avoid arguing with those who are unreceptive and remember that whenever the gospel is preached in simplicity and power, the Holy Spirit will convict the hearers of their sin and their need for Christ. Also, the testimony of a changed life is a powerful witness to the unbeliever, whether or not he will admit it. If you witness on a college campus, you should try to develop relationships with the local campus ministries, and encourage them to get involved in evangelism and follow-up.

9

Witnessing to Different Kinds of People

In this chapter, I want to give some suggestions for witnessing to children, young people, elderly people, Catholics and Jews. Most of this information is borrowed from other sources.

1. Witnessing to children

Children are generally very receptive to God's Word. Many have never heard the gospel before. Children are trusting, sensitive, and teachable. Also, children are hungry for love. Generally, they will first come to love their Bible teacher. Next, they will love their teacher's Bible. Finally, they will get to know and love their teacher's Lord.

I recommend that anyone seriously interested in witnessing to children contact Child Evangelism Fellowship (Warrenton, MO 63383) or some similar ministry. They can give you valuable training and ideas for reaching children.

Visual aids are very useful in reaching children. Explain God's Word simply and clearly. It helps to stress family relationships. When we are born of God, we become His child and He is our father. If the child does not have a good father, we need to explain that God loves him very much and wants to be a good father to him. He will never leave him or mistreat him.

Never force a child to receive Christ. Make sure the child understands what he is doing before he prays for salvation. If he does pray, encourage him to tell someone else what he did as soon as possible. Also, give him some verses about how he can have assurance of his salvation.

Some things we need to explain to children (and adults as well):

1. God is both holy and loving.
2. All of us have sinned (Isa. 53:6; Romans 3:23).
3. The wages of sin is death. Sin must be punished. We can't get rid of our own sin (Romans 6:23).
4. Jesus took the punishment for our sin. He died in our place, for the sins of the whole world (Isa.53:6b; John 3:16).
5. We must by our choice believe this and receive Him as our Savior. We can say yes or no to Him.
6. When we receive Him, He gives us the gift of eternal life. God becomes our heavenly Father. We receive this life in our spirit. You can't see your spirit, but it is like a little pocket inside you.
7. We can know from God's Word that we have been born again, that our sins have been forgiven (1 John 5:12).
8. After that, when we do something wrong, we must ask Him to forgive us right away. We do not lose His life, but are naughty children.
9. He wants us to grow to be like Him — kind, loving, helpful, ready to tell others about Him.
10. We grow by reading God's Word, praying, going to Bible classes, and telling others about Jesus.

If you pray with a group of children, have them close their eyes so they aren't looking at one another. Stress that they are making an individual choice. You can have them raise their hands to let you know what they have done. Afterwards, talk to them individually to make sure they understand what they are doing. Explain to them how they can know they are God's children.

If a child has truly received Christ, you should see a change in his life. He should show a desire to turn from sin and be right with God, a love for the Bible, a desire to witness to others, and an interest in church and Bible class. If he doesn't show these changes, pray that the Holy Spirit will do this work in his life, and talk with him about how Jesus expects him to grow and become more like Him. It he still does not show change, explain the plan of salvation to him again, and urge him to make a new commitment to Christ.

2. Witnessing to youth

Young people are looking for love and their own identity. Their consciences can still be touched. Usually, they desire reality with God and are aware of their sin. Many have been influenced by the unbelief of teachers and the media. They may want to analyze everything and put God in a test tube. However, they have not yet had time to develop a permanent philosophy and tend to change their views from time to time. "What is your opinion of Christ?" is a good opener.

Be yourself. Don't put on a front. Be straightforward in talking with young people, while being sensitive to develop a healthy relationship with them. Avoid putting down other religions. Share what Jesus has done for you.

If possible, talk to a person alone. Peer pressure is a powerful influence. Get the person involved. Let him ask questions. Give direct, simple answers. Keep an attitude of loving concern, even if the person is hard. Avoid lecturing him.

3. Witnessing to the elderly

Do not let statistics influence you against witnessing to the elderly. God is able to save people of all ages. Show an interest and listen to him. Often, older people feel (and are) forgotten.

1. Speak slowly and clearly in a normal tone of voice. If the person is hard of hearing, draw close and speak into the ear turned toward you. Repeat yourself if he doesn't seem to hear clearly what you are saying. Speak in a cheerful tone of voice.

2. Don't talk as if they are nearing death. You can share the gift of eternal life, but don't plan to bury them. Avoid depressing subjects. Dwell on the bright future in heaven offered to them.

3. Be a good listener. Older people like to talk about their past. You may be the first person who has listened to them in a long time. Look for opportunities to relate to them about their past Christian influences in church or Sunday School. Their childhood memories of early touches of faith can help them relate to God again. Also, resentment and guilt often keep them from receiving Christ.

4. While our purpose is to build a relationship, remember that you could be one of the last persons to share Christ with this person, especially if he is ill. This should not be seen as "operation desperation," but do be aware of God's timing with this person.

4. Witnessing to Catholics

Because of many doctrinal similarities, such as heaven, hell, repentance, the Trinity, etc., Roman Catholics are among the easiest people to bring to a "living relationship" with Jesus. Many Catholics have rejected the traditions of their church, yet still have a fear of God and a desire to know Him. Below are some common Catholic excuses with Biblical answers:

1. "It's not necessary that I read the Bible." Answer: 2 Tim. 2:15.

2. "I must suffer for my sins." Answer: Is it fair that two people suffer for your sins? 1 Peter 3:18.

3. "I can't get to heaven until I first go to purgatory." Answer: Are the flames of purgatory stronger than the blood of Jesus? 1 John 1:7.

4. "I hope to make heaven with my good works." Answer: Then Jesus' death was a horrible mistake. Eph. 2:8-9.

5. "No one can know he is going to heaven." Answer: If God said you could know, would you believe *Him*? 1 John 5:13.

6. "Well, don't you ever sin?" Answer: I no longer make a practice of it. 1 John 3:9.

7. "Do you believe in the saints?" Answer: Yes, I even read their writings daily — St. Matthew, St. Peter, St. Paul, etc.

8. "Do you believe in Mary?" Answer: Yes, Mary was honored by God, but she did not die on the cross for our sins. Acts

4:12.

9. "We pray to Mary so she can ask Jesus." Answer: If you needed an operation, would you go to the doctor or the doctor's mother? 1 Tim. 2:5.

10. "Do you believe in confession?" Answer: Yes, and the Bible is very clear as to whom I am to confess. 1 John 1:9; James 5:16.

11. "We Catholics belong to the true church." Answer: Surely you don't believe that every non-Catholic will go to hell. John 5:24.

5. *Witnessing to Jews*

In Romans 10 and 11, Paul speaks of God's plan to provoke the Jews to anger and jealousy through the Gentiles. The Gentiles have certainly provoked the Jews to anger over the years, but seldom to jealousy. If Jews can see the relationship that Gentiles have with their God, the joy and peace they have through knowing Him and reading His Word, and the love they have for the Jewish people, they will be provoked to jealousy.

Many Jews today are not religious and most have little knowledge of the Bible. If you win their confidence by your genuine love and concern for them, they will listen to what you say. Avoid arguing. It is easy to win the argument but lose the contact.

Some misconceptions Jews have of Christians:

1. Every Gentile is a Christian.
2. Christians killed six million Jews in Europe.
3. To be Christian is to cease being Jewish.
4. Christians worship three gods.
5. The Messiah didn't come to die; hence, he hasn't come yet.

Show your love and appreciation for the Jewish people. "I want to thank you and your nation for the Bible. Every writer was Jewish except possibly Luke. Without your Jewish Bible I'd be lost. I want to thank you for giving me your Messiah. I found atonement for my sins when I asked the Jewish Messiah into my life."

If he expresses doubt about Jesus being the Messiah, ask

him, "How would you recognize the Messiah if He were to appear right now?" Then open your Bible and read Isaiah 53:3-6. Ask him who he thinks this is talking about. Don't let him know you are reading from the Old Testament until after you have read the passage. Point out that Isaiah was an Old Testament prophet who wrote 700 years before Christ. Then read Isaiah 9:6 which speaks of a Son being born who is to be called "mighty God." Since Jews firmly believe that there is only one God, they stumble over the idea of God having a Son. Reading Proverbs 30:4 may help.

Old Testament prophecies with New Testament fulfillments are powerful witnesses to the Jew, even if he is not religious. Use a few that are clear rather than ones that are debatable. Only share as he is ready to listen. Don't "cram scriptures down his throat."

1. Born in Bethlehem. Micah 5:2; Matt. 2:1.
2. Miracle of a virgin birth. Isa. 7:14; Matt. 1:18.
3. Betrayed for 30 pieces of silver. Zech. 11:12; Matt. 26:15.
4. Side to be pierced. Zech. 12:10; John 19:34.
5. Pierced his hands and feet. Psalm 22:16 (read vv.1-18).
6. Blood cleansing for our sins. Isa. 53:5,6; John 1:29.

You can also explain how the Old Testament required blood sacrifices for sin, and how Christ is our atonement. Also, share about the Jewish passover, how the angel of death passed over the Jewish houses when the blood of the lamb was on their door. Jesus was called the Lamb of God.

Be patient in witnessing to Jews. They may argue and seem not to respond, but God may be working deeply in their lives. Also, remember that for a Jew to openly confess Jesus as Messiah probably means rejection by family and friends. Encourage them to count the cost, but let them know that the rewards of coming to Jesus are worth far more than the price we must pay.

Witnessing to Cultists

There are thousands of cults, occult groups, and new age groups involving millions of people. There are also hundreds of "aberrant Christian groups" that practice extreme psychological manipulation on their members or have serious doctrinal errors. I cannot discuss all these groups in this book. There are many good books on this subject in Christian bookstores. For more information, I suggest you contact two ministries that specialize in this area: Christian Research Institute, Box 500, San Juan Capistrano, CA 92693 and Spiritual Counterfeits Project, Box 4308, Berkeley, CA 94704. Each will send you a catalog of literature and answer specific questions.

One thing to realize when you talk with cultists is that often they use the same language we do, but it means something totally different to them. Often, they redefine terms like "resurrection" and "born again." In witnessing to cultists, you should get some basic information about their beliefs and how they differ from our beliefs. Otherwise, you could talk to someone in Christian Science, Mormonism, or the Unification Church (Rev. Moon) and think he believes what we do. To witness to a cultist, we need to know what we believe (especially such concepts as the Trinity) and why. At the same time, we should remember that our witness to cultists involves both reasoning with them from the scriptures and showing them the reality of our relationship with Jesus Christ.

10 ————————————————————

Witnessing to Homosexuals

Most of us have heard testimonies of people saved from drugs or prostitution. However, many Christians wonder if it is possible for a homosexual to be saved. Churches have debated this issue. Some have concluded that homosexuality is not a sin, that homosexuals are born that way and cannot change. The church, they say, should accept them as they are. Others have taken the opposite position — that homosexuals are reprobates and can't be saved, so we should keep them out of the church and not try to reach them. Many a homosexual has gone to his pastor for counsel, only to be thrown out of the church and have his sin announced publicly. Others were told that homosexuality is a "gift from God" and they should not resist these desires. Some have been seduced by their pastor or youth leader.

In recent years, many homosexuals have come "out of the closet." Every major city has a visible "gay" community. In almost every large church, some members will be struggling with this problem. I have known of pastors and youth leaders in evangelical churches who have left their family and church for a homosexual lover. While a prominent local pastor was crusading against homosexuality, his daughter — unknown to him — was a lesbian. The church can no longer ignore this issue.

1. Homophobia

Homophobia means "fear of homosexuality." In our society, men often grow up insecure about their sexual identity. They feel they have to go to bed with a woman to prove they aren't homosexual. We accept the idea of women embracing or kissing one another, or even sleeping in the same bed. Men are often afraid of showing any emotion toward someone of the same sex. Teenagers commonly call anyone they don't like a faggot or queer.

For many Christians, the hatred of homosexuality is based more upon their personal insecurities than a godly hatred of sin. We should hate all sin — especially the sin in our own life. We must not be self-righteous in witnessing to the homosexual. How did Jesus witness to the Samaritan woman? He looked at her as a valuable person, created in God's image, not as a "filthy prostitute."

"There is no temptation . . . but such as is common to man" (1 Cor. 10:13). Jesus "was in all ways tempted just as we are, only without sin" (Heb. 4:15). "Brethren, if a man be overtaken in a fault, you who are spiritual, restore such a one in the spirit of meekness, considering yourself, lest you also be tempted" (Gal. 6:1).

2. Causes of homosexuality

What causes homosexuality? This is a very complex issue. There is no proof that heredity or hormones are involved. Family background seems to be a factor, but one man may be homosexual while his brother is straight. Most homosexuals come from a family where the father is emotionally or physically absent. This is also true, however, of alcoholics and drug addicts. For male homosexuals, the mother was often dominant while the father was submissive. Many were victims of sexual abuse as a child. Many lesbians were beaten or raped by their fathers. Adolescent homosexual experimentation does not necessarily lead to homosexuality in adults.

3. What the Bible says about homosexuality

In the beginning, God created Adam and Eve. "And the Lord God said, it is not good that the man should be alone; I will make him a helper suitable for him . . . Therefore shall a man leave his father and mother, and cleave unto his wife: and they shall be one flesh" (Gen. 2:18,24). God did not make a second man, but rather a woman.

In the law given to Moses, God makes it very clear that homosexuality is sinful. "If a man also lie with mankind, as he lies with a woman, both of them have committed an abomination: they shall surely be put to death" (Lev. 20:13).

In the New Testament, homosexuality is always considered sinful. "For this cause God gave them unto vile affections: for even their women did change the natural use into that which is against nature: And likewise also the men, leaving the natural use of the woman, burned in their lust one toward another; men with men working that which is unseemly, and receiving in themselves the due penalty of their error" (Romans 1:26-27).

"Do you not know that the unrighteous shall not inherit the kingdom of God? Do not be deceived, neither fornicators . . . nor effeminate, nor homosexuals . . . shall inherit the kingdom of God. And such were some of you; but you were washed, but you were sanctified, but you were justified in the name of the Lord Jesus Christ" (1 Cor. 6:9-11). This passage, which condemns homosexual activity in the clearest terms, also offers hope. Some of the Corinthian church had been involved in homosexuality, and saved out of it. Actually, homosexuality was probably more common in the Greek and Roman society than it is today.

Despite these passages, there are those who maintain that homosexual activity is not sinful. They dismiss Leviticus 18 as "Old Testament." Romans 1, they say, is referring to heterosexuals who engage in homosexual activity, not true homosexuals. The Bible makes no such distinction. As Peter wrote, "the untaught and unstable distort (the writings of Paul) as they do also the other scriptures, unto their own destruction" (2 Peter 3:16). If a person wants badly enough to believe that homosexual behavior is not sinful, he will find a way to distort the Scriptures to agree with his position.

4. Coming out of homosexuality

Frank Worthen is director of Love in Action Ministry in San Rafael, twenty miles north of San Francisco. Love in Action is a Christian ministry to homosexuals. Frank has spent much of the past ten years studying the subject, having been a practicing homosexual for over twenty years. He has identified four components of homosexuality: psychic response, behavior, identity, and lifestyle. Psychic response is what excites you sexually. Behavior is actual sexual activity. Identity is the label you give yourself — homosexual or heterosexual. Lifestyle includes such things as living in a homosexual neighborhood, having homosexual friends, and going to gay bars.

When a homosexual is saved, God normally deals first with his lifestyle and behavior. Leaving the lifestyle can involve getting a new job (e.g., if he was working in a gay bar), getting a new set of friends, and finding a new place to live (if he has gay roommates). This requires a deep commitment to Christ. Giving up homosexual behavior can also be very difficult. Temptations are everywhere. It really helps if he knows a Christian he can talk and pray with when he is being tempted.

As the ex-homosexual grows spiritually, God shows him that he has a new identity. He is no longer a homosexual, but a new creature in Christ. Psychic response is the hardest area to deal with. It is very hard to control our thought life. We need to fill our mind with godly thoughts. As Christians, we tend to have a double standard. If a heterosexual has lustful thoughts, we dismiss it as normal. If an ex-homosexual has lustful thoughts, we conclude that he isn't cured. In fact, sometimes we encourage him to replace homosexual lust with heterosexual lust.

All Christians are tempted by sexual lust. Only when we yield to temptation does it become sin. We can't prevent lustful thoughts from entering our mind, but we can refuse to dwell on these thoughts, and think instead on things that are true, honest, just, pure, lovely, and of good report (Phil. 4:8).

Healing for the ex-homosexual is generally a gradual process. As God deals with the root causes — pride, envy, self-pity, rejection, fear of or hatred toward women, etc. — healing will come in his life.

5. Witnessing to homosexuals

In a sense, witnessing to homosexuals is no different from witnessing to anyone else. We have one gospel to present to all people — gay or straight. We are not calling people to celibacy. We are telling them of their need to know Jesus Christ as Savior and Lord. Once they know Him, He will do the changing in their lives.

Usually, you don't need to bring up the issue of homosexuality. Most gay people will bring it up themselves. In response, we can briefly explain that homosexuality is a sin, but it is possible to put aside that lifestyle with God's help. Avoid getting sidetracked into a long argument about whether or not homosexuality is a sin. Ask the person if he would be willing to turn away from homosexuality if God showed him it was a sin and helped him to change. Then begin talking about other sin problems he may have — such as lying or unforgiveness. Many homosexuals are very much aware that their lifestyle is sinful, and want to change. You can assure them that change is possible with God's help.

In San Francisco, we have experienced a great deal of opposition from some homosexuals who do not want the gospel preached in "their community." As the gay rights movement spreads, you can expect increased hostility to the gospel by homosexuals throughout the country. We need to reach these people now, before they become more hardened to God's Word.

Christians from a homosexual background need to be very careful about witnessing to gays. Some ex-homosexuals who have come to San Francisco to witness have fallen into sin. An ex-gay should examine himself realistically to see if he is ready for this kind of ministry. Generally, I recommend that the person be out of active homosexual involvement at least a year. Even then, it is quite possible to fall. He should not witness by himself, but go with a strong Christian brother or sister. He needs to be especially careful witnessing near old hangouts and to old friends and lovers.

You don't need to come from a homosexual background to witness to gays. In fact, straight Christians have a great advantage — they aren't tempted by homosexual lust. Many gays really want a heterosexual friend who will love and accept them. Many would like to marry and live a "normal" life. Be yourself, show love to the homosexual, and share honestly about your own sexual temptations and how God is helping you with them.

Finally, don't neglect follow-up. When the homosexual prays to receive Christ, you need to do all you can to help him grow spiritually. This means spending time with him, taking him to church, helping him with problems and possibly helping him to find a new place to live. Although it's easy to get discouraged when someone you've ministered to falls back into sin, remember that God is still working in his life. Continue to pray for him.

Homosexuality is one of the most difficult things to come out of. Unfortunately, many people do go back into it. Often, it takes years of prayer, counseling, and God's dealing for a person to get free. Living in a Christian discipleship house can be helpful in many cases. Unfortunately, many house leaders do not know how to minister to homosexuals. Close Christians friendships and church involvement are also very helpful, but many Christians do not feel comfortable relating to ex-homosexuals. I hope that this chapter will help you understand homosexuality better, so God can use you to reach homosexuals with the gospel.

Love in Action Ministry, which I mentioned earlier, is part of a network of Christian ministries to homosexuals called Exodus International. They can provide helpful literature on various topics related to homosexuality, as well as provide counseling for those struggling with homosexuality. They can also refer you to an ex-gay ministry in your area. Most of the people in these ministries have come out of homosexuality, and understand what is involved in getting victory over it. Exodus can be reached at P O Box 2121, San Rafael, CA 94912, (415) 454-0960.

11 _____

Signs and Wonders in Street Evangelism

There is a lot of debate in the church about the place of signs and wonders in evangelism. I believe that we can err by either underemphasizing or overemphasizing their importance. At one extreme, some Christians deny that God works miracles today or say that such miracles are irrelevant to the gospel. At the other extreme, some Christians believe that there is no value in preaching the gospel unless it is accompanied by signs and wonders.

Jesus performed many miracles and He commanded his disciples to heal the sick, raise the dead, and cast out demons. However, despite all of Jesus' miracles, many refused to believe. Several times Jesus reproved those who were seeking after signs instead of believing His Word. We are commanded to preach the gospel, and people will be held accountable for what they have heard, regardless of whether they see a miracle.

If we are to witness effectively for the Lord, we need to go in the power of the Holy Spirit. The book of Acts is filled with examples of how in the early church, the preaching of God's Word was confirmed with signs following. As a result, the world of their day was turned "upside down." In Acts chapter 3, Peter and John saw a lame man sitting outside the temple, asking for money. When they told him to "rise up and walk," and he did, it had a tremendous effect on all those who had seen this miracle. While some opposed the gospel, many others were saved.

Such miracles were common in the early church. Faced with opposition, the early believers prayed "that with all boldness they may speak your word, by stretching forth your hand to heal, and that signs and wonders may be done by the name of your holy child Jesus" (Acts 4:29-30). Not just the apostles did miracles. "Stephen, full of faith and power, did great wonders and miracles among the people" (Acts 6:8).

Often, the miracles recorded in the book of Acts resulted in many people being saved. After Peter raised Dorcas from the dead, "it was known throughout all Joppa, and many believed in the Lord" (Acts 9:42). When Elymus sought to oppose the gospel, Paul told him that he would be blind for a season. When the local deputy saw this, he believed, "being astonished at the doctrine of the Lord" (Acts 13:12). Paul told the Corinthians that his preaching was not "with enticing words of man's wisdom, but in demonstration of the Spirit and of power" (1 Cor. 2:4). The gospel message was being demonstrated with power. How we need this power in today's unbelieving world!

The book of Acts is filled with such examples. Philip was supernaturally caught away after witnessing to the Ethiopian eunuch. The Lord Jesus appeared to Saul as he was on his way to persecute Christians. Ananias prayed for him to receive his sight. Peter was released from prison by an angel of God. "God did special miracles by the hands of Paul, so that from his body were brought unto the sick handkerchiefs or aprons, and the diseases departed from them, and the evil spirits went out of them" (Acts 19:11-12).

Many people today are asking, "Why don't I see these things happening today?" Some have argued that these miracles were only for the early church. While this is a convenient excuse for our powerlessness, I do not believe that the position can be justified scripturally. Throughout church history, there have been many documented cases of healings and miracles. After the first century, these miracles seem to have become infrequent until the twentieth century. Today, many healings and miracles are reported in other countries and in healing services in this country. Recently, a number of healings are being reported in response to a word of knowledge given over Christian television. However, we still hear of very few miracles occurring on the streets in the United States.

In the Bible, healings and miracles generally took place outdoors, in public places. When the lame man was healed outside the Temple in Acts 3, it was a witness to all the people who had seen that man begging every day. People today are skeptical of healing services and Christian TV. But when the beggar with no legs they have seen on the street for many years is healed in the name of Jesus, it will be hard to deny that a miracle has occurred.

In 1985, we had an outdoor concert scheduled at Hallidie Plaza, near the cable car turnaround at Powell St. About 300,000 people pass through that area each day. This day, we had joined with Jerry Brandt, an evangelist who was involved with singles ministries in Northern California.

Jerry told me that God had spoken to him to have a healing service that day. So Jerry announced that we were having a healing service and that all those who needed healing should come forward at that time. People started coming and as we prayed for them, several told us they were healed. Cameramen from a local Christian TV station were filming the outreach, and they filmed some of the prayer and testimonies.

On that day, we did not get the names and addresses of the people involved and obtain medical verifications for healings. Whenever possible, we should attempt to get such confirmations. Not every person who claims to be healed really has been healed. Most unbelievers and many Christians are extremely skeptical of divine healing.

I believe that God is eager to confirm His Word with signs and wonders. We should pray for people's needs and give God opportunities to heal them. Also, we need to be sensitive to what God wants to do in a situation. As we learn to hear His voice, we will see more healings and other miracles.

We live in a very skeptical age. While miracles will not convince everyone, some people will only believe in Christ when they see His power being manifested through signs and wonders. Our evangelistic methods are no substitute for God's power. It takes the power of the Holy Spirit to bring people to Christ.

Many of us will readily admit that our greatest weakness is in the area of prayer (and fasting). If a need arises, we will think of a way to meet it ourselves, rather than go to God with that need. Too often, our prayer life lacks in consistency, fervency, and faith. Most of us know little about real intercession and travailing in prayer. We read about men and women who have been greatly used of God in the past. Invariably they were prayer warriors. The great spiritual revivals of the past were the result of much prayer. We know the great need for revival in our day — the great wickedness all around us, the shortage of gospel workers around the world, the hardness of hearts to the gospel, the many countries that are closed to missionaries, the lack of signs and wonders confirming our witness, the indifference of God's people — yet our prayers are half-hearted. We need to cry out to God to revive us.

Also, we need to ask for the gifts of the Holy Spirit related to miracles: the word of knowledge, the gift of faith, the gifts of healing, the working of miracles, prophecy, and the discerning of spirits. When we witness on the streets, we should ask people if they have a need we can pray for, and pray for them right there. If you don't see an immediate answer, write down the request and continue to pray for them. At first, you may not have a lot of success, but if you persevere, you will begin to see results. I am convinced that God greatly desires to manifest His power on our streets, that many would turn to Him.

12

Dealing with Opposition

We are in a spiritual battle, and Satan will do anything he can to keep us from witnessing and to destroy our street witnessing teams. "We are not ignorant of his (Satan's) devices" (2 Cor. 2:11). One thing Satan will do is get us discouraged or depressed. Perhaps we aren't seeing as many results on the street as we would like. Perhaps someone who came to Christ and was growing in the Lord suddenly backslides. Satan may attack you or others in your group with personal problems, such as financial problems or sickness. Division is another tool of the enemy. A witnessing team, like a church, may split apart due to differences in methodology or doctrine.

Other Christians may say that your methods are wrong, that you are "turning people off" to God's Word. Unbelievers, as we would expect, may not want us to witness publicly for the Lord. It causes them to be convicted of their sin, ruins their fun and makes them feel uncomfortable. They may yell at us, tear up our tracts, try to ignore us, or criticize us. Sometimes they will misuse Bible verses such as "don't do your alms before men" or "judge not." Some unbelievers may threaten us with violence, or even organize to get us off the streets.

In the fourteen years I have been involved in street witnessing with thousands of other Christians, I have never seen anyone injured in any serious way. San Francisco contains an unusually large number of people who oppose God's Word.

People have been slapped, spit upon and hit. Proverbs 15:1 says, "a soft answer turns away wrath." Those few who were hit often were not using much wisdom in the things they said to angry people. We have seen some organized opposition to our witnessing from the large homosexual community. Opposition can also come from the police and legal system. Often, the police are responding to complaints from citizens.

How do we deal with these attacks? Let me give four steps to use:

1. Remember that tribulation is an integral part of the Christian life. Read 2 Cor. 11 about the things Paul went through — beatings, shipwreck, perils by his own countrymen, perils by the heathen, perils by false brethren.

2. Recognize the source of these attacks – Satan.

3. Pray both individually and with other Christians. Come against Satan in Jesus' name. Ask the Lord for wisdom (James 1) and deliverance. Fasting is a powerful weapon in spiritual warfare, as is praise and worship. "In every thing give thanks" (1 Thess. 5:18). Remember that Satan can do nothing without God's permission (Job 1). Even if you do not understand at the time, God has a purpose in each trial, to strengthen your faith (Romans 5:1-5; James 1, 4:6-10).

4. Make a commitment to the Lord to continue witnessing despite all attacks. As much as is possible, continue witnessing with your team (as many as show up) every week, no matter how you feel or what the weather is like (unless it is so bad that nobody will be on the streets). Satan's purpose in attacking you is to persuade you to give up. Once he knows you aren't going to stop, he will have to try something else. Focus on the Lord, His love and His strength, not on your circumstances, Satan, or your own personal weaknesses.

In dealing with attacks from within your witnessing team, the key is to respond in love and humility. If God has put you in leadership, He will establish and maintain your authority. Don't be a lord over others. Be a servant. As problems arise in your group, take them to God in prayer. Pray for the other members of your witnessing team. Satan will be attacking them as well as you. Phone them, invite them to dinner, and encourage them in their spiritual growth. Avoid things that make for disunity, especially divisive arguments about doctrines that are not central to salvation. Don't expect everyone to witness in the same way.

God may direct one person to preach boldly about God's righteous standards and our sinful condition. He may lead another person to witness gently, establishing friendships with people and gradually sharing about Christ. You may need to instruct the bold preacher not to be unnecessarily offensive and harsh, or the gentle witnesser not to compromise the truth. But we need to be open to God's Spirit leading people in ways we do not understand, and also be patient with our Christian brethren, realizing that change is usually a slow process. On rare occasions, you may need to remove someone from your witnessing team who consistently refuses to submit to leadership, is divisive, or seriously hinders your work in some other way. Most of the Christians who join your witnessing team are there because they love God and want to serve Him, and they will support you in your efforts to work out any problem that arises in the team.

While you are on the streets, you may meet Christians who criticize you, usually for your methods. Again, it is important to respond in love and humility. These Christians may never have seen a street preacher before. We need to instruct them in meekness concerning what the Bible says about witnessing. If they want to argue with you about some doctrine not essential to salvation, explain to them that you are on the streets to witness to the lost, not to argue doctrine. Don't spend a lot of time with a Christian unless he needs and responds to your counsel and encouragement.

In San Francisco, we have experienced a lot of opposition, probably much more than you are likely to experience in your community. San Francisco has a reputation as a center of various types of immorality. Everyone does what is right in his own eyes, and there is no consensus as to what is right or wrong. Many people come to San Francisco to get away from God and Christian morality, to escape from the "Bible belt." San Francisco also has a very large and politically influential homosexual community, many of whom are quite hostile to Christianity.

They have formed "gay churches" that say homosexuality is not a sin.

When we first started witnessing in the homosexual neighborhoods, we faced a great deal of opposition. People threatened us, harrassed us, even organized special committees to drive us off the street. The homosexual papers called us "anti-gay bigots" and many worse things. Several times, small groups of Christians were surrounded by angry mobs. In each situation, God protected us and showed us what to do.

During our first SOS-San Francisco outreach in 1980, about fifty Christians were surrounded by several hundred angry homosexuals on Castro Street, the center of militant homosexuality in San Francisco. We were worshipping the Lord and God showed us to keep worshipping Him, as a witness to the people who were mocking us. After about an hour, we were able to leave peacefully. Nobody was hurt.

The next year, a massive effort was made by the homosexual leaders to stop the work of our ministry. Several thousand people came against about five hundred Christians at one of our rallies. But God had prepared us for the opposition. He instructed us to do nothing but worship Him, and not to respond to their attacks. For two hours, we worshipped God, singing a few choruses over and over. Those who were opposing blew whistles in our ears, tore up tracts and Bibles, even tried to destroy the P.A. system.

The police were there with riot gear and were ready to intervene. Finally, we began to sing "Oh, the blood of Jesus." As we sang that song, the whistle noise died down. People started to walk away. The officer in charge of the riot squad said, "Keep singing that song. It's changing things." Nobody was hurt that day. Some of those who had opposed us told us later that they were ashamed of their activities.

The organization that led the opposition was torn apart by division the next year, and has stopped fighting our work. Since that time, we have experienced no organized opposition on the streets of San Francisco, even in the homosexual neighborhoods.

As Christians, we should be willing to die, if necessary, for

Jesus Christ. One day we may see martyrdom in this country. Right now, most persecution is mild. What we went through was a bit scary, but nobody was hurt. Unfortunately, even the possibility of violence is enough to scare off most Christians in this country. Satan will use our fears to keep us from witnessing. There is an old saying that "a coward dies a thousand deaths, a hero only one."

A while back, a man threatened to burn down our ministry house. At first, I was fearful, but as I prayed God gave me perfect peace in the matter. Since then, he made threats to other Christians, but never carried them out. However, he succeeded in scaring off some of our workers, and they never came out witnessing again. We need to remember that our life is not our own; we belong to Christ. I would rather die preaching God's Word than live in constant fear. God wants to take away our fears and give us boldness to continue witnessing for Him. "Perfect love casts out fear" — love for God and love for the lost.

Usually, we will find the greatest opposition when we first start witnessing in a certain neighborhood. Satan will fight to keep the people in that area under his control. People may get upset, or think what you are doing is illegal since they've never seen anyone witness there before. The police may give you trouble, especially if they get complaints. Like the children of Israel entering the promised land, we need to fight (with spiritual weapons) to gain ground for Jesus Christ. When we faced great opposition in the homosexual neighborhoods, God showed us that our weapons are praise, worship, prayer, love, and humility. There is no way Satan can fight against these weapons.

The Bible says in Romans 13 that the police are ordained of God to protect those who do good and to punish evildoers. If someone persists in harrassing Christians, you may need to call the police or even get a restraining order against the person. Usually, a warning from a policeman is sufficient to end harrassment.

We need to know our rights under the law. *Take Him To The Streets* has an excellent chapter on street preaching legalities.

Paul made use of his legal rights several times, such as when he appealed as a Roman citizen to Caesar. Even if the law did not support our right to preach the gospel, "we must obey God rather than men" (Acts 5:29). We should not be arrogant in demanding our rights, but act in humility and with respect towards those in authority. "The wrath of man does not work the righteousness of God" (James 1:20).

If you run into opposition from a policeman, write down his name and badge number. The next day call the police captain, the city attorney or the chief of police. Explain to him what you are doing, and how you believe you are acting within your First Amendment rights. If you can't handle the situation over the phone, arrange an appointment. If possible, bring a Christian lawyer with you, or have him write a letter for you. Usually, this will take care of the problem.

In rare instances you may need to go to court. Get a lawyer — preferably Christian — and talk with him before doing anything. Don't be quick to get involved in legal controversy, as it will distract you from the work of preaching God's Word. Use it only as a last resort. But God may want you to go to court in order to open up your city to the preaching of the gospel for all Christians. If you do, the legal precedents are clear about our rights to preach, assemble, and distribute literature in public places.

Let me give a word of caution: If you are persecuted, make sure it is for Christ, not for your wrongdoing. If you call people names, or scream in their ears, you can expect them to be angry.

Dealing with Rejection

One thing that is certain whenever you preach is that you will face rejection. Many people will not welcome your witness. When they hear about Jesus, the Holy Spirit starts convicting them of sins. If they are not willing to repent at that time, this will make them feel uncomfortable and often they will take it out on you. "Get away, you Jesus freak. Stop trying to put a guilt trip on me." They are trying to get around the discomfort they are feeling, and at the same time, Satan is using them to discourage you from witnessing.

Most of us are insecure. We actively seek the approval of others. We actively avoid rejection. We have heard that these people are not rejecting us, they are rejecting the Lord. This is true. Nonetheless, we don't like it when people reject us or our Lord. Many Christians start to witness actively for the Lord, but the repeated rejection they experience gradually takes its toll on them. Before long, they find they just don't want to go witnessing any more. They know they should witness. They feel guilty about not witnessing. But they won't do it.

The continued rejection and the subtle attacks of Satan have accomplished their purpose. We feel like we're spoiling people's fun, we're pushing our trip on them, we're witnessing the wrong way, these people don't want to hear anyway, or they've already heard enough and we should just pray for them. Satan will give us a thousand reasons to stop witnessing.

We have all heard that God has a plan for our lives. Satan also has a plan for our lives. His plan has two parts: 1) to keep us from getting saved and 2) having failed at that, to keep us from leading others to Christ. He has two ways of accomplishing his second purpose: 1) to cause us to lead defeated lives so we will feel unworthy of witnessing and 2) to give us various excuses for not witnessing. It is evident that Satan has been very successful at accomplishing this second purpose.

God's desire for us, the church, is that we be an overcoming army. We need to be aware of the enemy's tactics and not be overcome by them. We need to remember that we are in a war, that our goal is to rescue those who have been held captive by the enemy and bring them into God's kingdom. We must be strong in the Lord. Sure, it hurts to be rejected and insulted. But we can rejoice that we are partakers of Christ's sufferings. He was insulted. He was misunderstood. Even Peter tried to dissuade Him from going to the cross. Our Christian brethren may try to persuade us not to obey Christ's commission to take His Word into all the world. But God will be with us, and strengthen us, as we take a stand for Him despite all opposition.

Dealing with Discouragement

Everyone who is involved in Christian ministry will experience times of discouragement. After Elijah's great victory over the prophets of Baal, he ran into the wilderness after being threatened by Jezebel. He felt that he was the only one left who was faithful to God, but God assured him that he had 7000 left who had not bowed the knee to Baal (1 Kings 19:18).

The ministry of Paul the apostle had its moments of victory, but largely it was one of tremendous suffering and opposition. He was beaten at least eight times, stoned, shipwrecked, and spent many years in prison. Other Christians questioned his apostleship and several of his closest friends deserted him. When Paul and Silas were jailed at Philippi, at midnight they were singing praises to God. Paul wrote most of his epistles from jail, yet they are filled with joy and encouragement. At the end of his life, Paul wrote from prison, "At my first defense, no man stood with me, but all men forsook me: I pray God that it may not be laid to their charge. Notwithstanding the Lord stood with me, and strengthened me" (2 Tim. 4:16-17).

The Bible promises us that if we are to serve God we will suffer persecution, afflictions and tribulations. We will be rejected by the world and often also by other Christians. There will be times when we won't understand why God does something or doesn't answer some prayer. Peter writes us, "Think it not strange concerning the fiery trial which is to try you, as though some strange thing happened unto you; But rejoice, inasmuch as you are partakers of Christ's sufferings" (1 Peter 4:12-13).

Many American Christians have been taught, and come to expect, that the Christian life will be easy, that problems should be small and easily overcome through faith in Christ. When persecution comes from preaching, they think they must be outside God's will so they stop witnessing. "All who will live godly in Christ Jesus shall suffer persecution" (2 Tim. 3:12).

True disciples of Christ have always known that the Christian life is not easy. In fact, it is *very hard*. It will include much persecution, afflictions and suffering. There will be times of disappointments and discouragement. Yet we must persevere in the work God has called us to do.

Here are some things that will help you deal with discouragement:

1. Know what God has called you to do. Seek God in prayer and His Word. Fast and pray for direction. Once you know what God wants you to do, continue to fulfill that vision regardless of circumstances.

2. Learn to praise God in all circumstances. "A merry heart does good like a medicine" (Prov. 17:22). Remember how Paul and Silas were in prison singing praises to God when the earthquake came.

3. Avoid "formula Christianity." Every Christian who sings praises at midnight in a prison won't be delivered by an earthquake. When we expect God to act according to our formulas, we set ourselves up for disappointments. We need to consider God's promises in context and in light of His entire Word.

4. Expect hardships, disappointments and persecutions. God promises that we will experience them. As Peter said, don't be surprised when they occur.

5. Avoid self-pity. Get involved in serving and praying for others. At their worst, our problems are small compared to those of the unsaved. We have much to thank God for. His greatest gift to us, of course, is our salvation.

6. Resist the devil. Discouragement is one of Satan's favorite tools. He tells us, as I'm sure he told the apostle Paul, that our work is in vain. Remember that Satan is a liar.

7. Remember our hope in Christ. Throughout history, godly people have realized that their hope is in the return of Christ and our living forever with Him. People may laugh about "pie in the sky when you die" but we know that our "blessed hope" is a sure one. Without it, there is no reason to endure the persecutions and sufferings we experience serving Christ.

Today, American Christians find that they can live a pretty comfortable life and avoid persecution by not witnessing for Christ or by watering down the gospel so it doesn't offend anyone. Many have fallen for this temptation. Don't let it happen to you.

"Endure hardship, as a good soldier of Jesus Christ. No man who wars entangles himself with the affairs of this life; that he may please him who has chosen him to be a soldier. And if a man competes as an athlete, he is not crowned unless he competes according to the rules. The farmer who labors should be the first to partake of the fruits." (2 Tim. 2:3-7).

13 ⎯⎯⎯⎯⎯⎯⎯⎯⎯⎯⎯⎯⎯⎯⎯⎯⎯⎯

How SOS Ministries Got Started

I was raised in a middle-class Jewish home in Indiana. We were very liberal in our beliefs. I was taught to believe in evolution and humanistic philosophy, at home, at school, and in the synagogue. As I was growing up, many of my friends called themselves Christians and I'm sure some were, but they never witnessed to me. One friend in high school invited me to some Youth for Christ meetings and I attended a few but still nobody explained the plan of salvation to me or invited me to receive Christ. I went to college and graduate school, taking classes in philosophy and psychology in my search to find the meaning of life. Later I got involved in drugs and Eastern religions as part of this search.

I was saved in 1970 through Shiloh Youth Revival Centers in Oregon, a ministry from "Jesus People" days with a nation-wide network of communal Christian houses. Everybody in our ministry witnessed on the streets, so I considered it a natural part of being a Christian. After I got over the initial fear, I loved to witness and did so at virtually every opportunity.

One thing God had given me was an intense burden for the lost. I got saved when I was 24 years old and this was the first time somebody had explained to me clearly what it meant to be born again. When I realized that the Bible is God's Word and

Jesus Christ is the only Savior for the world, I wondered why nobody told me this before. One other thing struck me — almost all my friends and most of the people I came in contact with each day were unsaved, and heading for an eternal hell. Someone needed to warn them.

In 1975, God called me to come to San Francisco and witness on the streets. I had lived in San Francisco before I was saved as a "hippie" and I always had a special burden for this city. My only plans were to get a part-time job and spend the rest of my time witnessing on the streets. I never expected to start a street ministry.

I started attending a local church that was known for being evangelistic. They had a full-time minister of evangelism and most of the church members had been through an extensive evangelism training program. As I met people in church, I would invite them to go witnessing with me. Usually they would agree, and we would set a time and meeting place. Almost every time, the person wouldn't show up. Finally, I realized that most of these Christians, even though they had received a lot of teaching on evangelism, had virtually no experience witnessing to strangers and were terribly afraid to do this.

Some Christians I knew had a band and they had started doing evangelistic concerts in parks. It seemed like a good way to reach a lot of people with God's Word at one time. So I found out how to get permits, borrowed a small P.A. system from a church, and asked some friends who had a Christian band to play at Union Square, a small park in downtown San Francisco.

During a single afternoon, several hundred people would walk through this park — businessmen, tourists, drug addicts, homosexuals, teenage runaways, prostitutes. When the Christian rock group started to play, they drew a good-sized crowd. People would eventually realize that these musicians were singing about Jesus, but most would stay because they liked the music. The musicians shared testimonies about how they got saved and someone would preach a short message. A local ministry called His Way gave us New Testaments to give away and people took as many as we had.

As we did these concerts, I met many Christians who thought this was a great idea, and wanted to be involved. One brother, Ron Woodruff, was doing outdoor concerts in the East Bay and had a large P.A. system. He also had contacts with other Christian bands, access to a computerized mailing list, a typesetting machine, and a Christian printer. Ron had just formed a non-profit corporation for his ministry called Shama Sound Ministries, Inc. ("Shama" comes from the Hebrew word meaning "to hear" or "to proclaim.") So we started printing up fliers advertising our concerts and mailing them to Christians as well as giving them out at Christian events.

In a short time, we met leaders of several churches in the San Francisco area who wanted to do evangelism outreaches in San Francisco. We would schedule a weekend outreach and each group would bring 30-50 Christians from their church. We got another 30-50 Christians from our mailings, bringing the total to about 200. On Friday and Saturday nights, we met at a church for worship and prayer, and then went to some area to witness. On Saturday at noon, we had an outdoor concert, usually at Union Square, and then witnessed downtown. We started writing and printing our own tracts.

After several years of organizing weekend outreaches like this, which involved 100-200 Christians every six weeks, twenty leaders who had been involved in planning these outreaches met together in January, 1980. At that meeting, we decided to plan a major, week-long outreach for August, which we called SOS-San Francisco. People are constantly asking us, "What does SOS stand for?" An SOS is a distress signal, a call for help. We wanted to send out an "SOS" to Christians all over the United States to come to San Francisco to witness for the Lord. People have suggested various meanings to the letters, but the only one I like is "Serve our Savior."

We printed up thousands of posters and other literature inviting Christians to the outreach. Our mailing list grew to 5000 and we mailed out newsletters all over the country. We set up booths and gave out fliers at every Christian event we could find. We shared about the outreach at churches and on Christian radio stations.

In July, David Wilkerson, founder of Teen Challenge ministry and now director of World Challenge, brought a team of thirty workers to San Francisco. They gave out 200,000 copies of a booklet David wrote called "Two of Me: the Struggle with Sin." They also established a Christian coffeehouse in the heart of the Tenderloin district, the skid-row area of San Francisco. This coffeehouse continued as an effective ministry for four years.

About 1500 Christians were involved in the first SOS-San Francisco outreach. Every day and night we sent teams of Christians throughout the city to witness for the Lord. We printed up and gave out about half a million tracts written specially for San Francisco. We put up hundreds of SOS posters around the city. Every afternoon we had an evangelistic concert in a downtown park. Everywhere people went that week in San Francisco, they were likely to run into Christians who would witness to them about Christ.

Looking back, I still marvel at the way God used some very ordinary Christians to establish a powerful street ministry in San Francisco. When God called me to San Francisco, I never expected to do anything but witness on the street with a few other Christians. I knew nothing about establishing a ministry, setting up a non-profit corporation, putting out newsletters, or coordinating evangelism outreaches involving hundreds of Christians. But after five years of witnessing on the streets, getting little response either from unbelievers or Christians, I became a leader of a ministry that was having a significant impact for Christ on one of the wickedest cities in the world.

14

A Brief History of SOS Ministries

The first SOS-San Francisco outreach in 1980 was the combined effort of several churches and ministries in Northern California. After this outreach, we felt that God was directing us to establish an ongoing ministry to San Francisco. At the time, the SOS steering committee consisted of twelve people:

1. Ron Woodruff. Ron and Wayne Conley founded Shama Sound Ministries, Inc., which became the corporation under which SOS Ministries operated. Ron and Wayne purchased a large P.A. system and began doing evangelistic concerts in the East Bay. In 1981, Ron moved to San Francisco to work with me full-time in SOS Ministries. Ron met his wife Jennifer at our 1984 outreach, and she is now the SOS secretary. Together, Ron and I oversee the work of SOS Ministries. We are very different in our gifts and temperament. Each of us tends to be strong in areas where the other is weak. Over the past eight years, we have gone through many struggles learning to work together, but God has used these to make us an effective team.

2. Michael Brodeur. Michael grew up in the Castro district of San Francisco as a "hippie child." Several years after he was saved, he came to San Francisco with a team from Gospel Outreach of Eureka, California. He worked with Ron and me organizing outreaches for several years before SOS Ministries was started. Michael is now pastor of the Vineyard Christian Fellowship of San Francisco and continues to work with SOS. Michael met his wife Diane at our first SOS-San Francisco outreach.

3. Darrell Walker and 4. Brad Byrum. Darrell and Brad were the leaders of Agape, Inc., a dynamic street ministry in San Francisco, affiliated with the Assemblies of God. They preached on the streets of San Francisco almost every day for several years. They also did a lot of outreach in the Tenderloin (skid row) district of San Francisco and operated the Candle coffeehouse (started by David Wilkerson) for many years. Darrell was killed in a car accident after our 1981 summer outreach. After that, Agape, Inc. became Agape Fellowship, a church fellowship for inner city people in San Francisco. In 1985, Brad took a leave of absence from ministry to go to school and Ron Woodruff became pastor of Agape Fellowship.

5. Gary Goodell. Gary was pastor of Faith Fellowship Foursquare Church in Oakland for many years before leaving in 1985 to pastor a Foursquare Church in Southern California. Gary has a real heart for street ministry and greatly helped us by providing wise counsel and by getting pastors involved with us.

6. Randy Sager. Randy was founder and pastor of the Fellowship of the Living God, Castro Valley. Randy taught us about the importance of praise and worship in evangelism. The worship group from his church led many of our worship rallies. The Fellowship has reorganized as the New Life Christian Church and the pastor, Dennis McNally, has been involved with SOS for several years.

7. Doug Shearer. Doug is founder of TAV Evangelical Ministries and co-pastor of New Hope Christian Fellowship in Sacramento. Doug has a tremendous ability to motivate Christians to witness for Christ. He regularly brings teams of Christians to San Francisco and the New Hope worship group leads worship at many of our rallies. TAV Ministries grew out of relationships that began in SOS. TAV is a Jewish outreach that has established dialogues between top Jewish and evangelical Christian leaders. TAV has also organized joint Jewish-Christian worship services which have been a powerful witness for Christ in the Jewish community. Doug is still very much involved with SOS Ministries.

8. Richard Paradise. In 1980, Richard was the pastor of the Russian River Christian Fellowship in Guerneville, CA. At the time, he brought teams from his church to witness with us in San Francisco. For many years, Richard was a leader in Gospel Outreach, a world-wide network of churches established during the Jesus Movement. Richard is now starting a ministry in Berkeley, New Horizons Ministries, and continues to work with SOS.

9. Scott Crawford. Scott has been an evangelist for many years, working with Resurrection City, a church founded by Mario Murillo in Berkeley. As Scott traveled around the country preaching, he met many other street preachers. Every year he went to New Orleans to witness at the Mardi Gras. A number of other Christians also went there, and they started a joint outreach. Scott's experiences there gave him the idea for a week-long outreach to San Francisco, and he also gave us the name "SOS-San Francisco." Scott also started a Christian house in San Francisco where Ron Woodruff, Michael Brodeur and I lived, which became the first headquarters for SOS Ministries. Scott is now the director of Evangelism for Jesus Ministries in Fort Bragg, California, and continues to work with SOS Ministries and the International Street Ministries Association (ISMA).

10. Gary Lukas. Gary is pastor of North Beach Christian Fellowship, a church located on Broadway Street, a tourist area that features topless bars, male strippers, and female impersonators. Gary has preached on that street faithfully for seven years, in addition to witnessing door-to-door, and at street fairs and parades in San Francisco.

11. Dan Russell. Dan was a pastor at Calvary Community Church in San Jose. He helped us greatly with the planning for our first two SOS outreaches and led a Youth With a Mission base in San Francisco for about a year.

12. Larry Rosenbaum. Everyone else was involved in another ministry besides SOS, so I ended up being the director of SOS Ministries, largely because I had the time to give to it.

We planned a second SOS-San Francisco outreach for 1981. During this year, opposition to us by the homosexual community became very intense. A city-funded organization called Community United Against Violence spearheaded a campaign against us in the homosexual press. Every week an article appeared which described us in the worst possible terms. "They harrass local citizens . . . They condemn minorities . . . They cause violence . . . They cry out for our extermination," said one flier. We became the targets of homosexual hostility towards Anita Bryant and Jerry Falwell, even though we carefully avoided any political statements. In an earlier chapter — "Dealing with Opposition" — I described how God gave us a great victory in the confrontation that took place that year.

In 1980, our ministry received a lot of criticism from San Francisco churches. In 1981, God showed us to reach out to these churches and serve them. That year, we were able to work with twenty local churches and establish an excellent relationship with them. We really needed that support from local churches when we met such great opposition from the militant homosexuals. We also put together a slide show about our ministry and showed it to about ten thousand Christians at fifty churches and several large Christian gatherings.

At the end of 1981, a Christian brother donated part of his equity in a San Francisco house, allowing us to buy the house that has become the center of our ministry. 1982 and 1983 were years of growth — getting our ministry established, raising up leaders, witnessing to many people and counseling new believers. In 1982, Jeff Harsh, a Christian businessman from Kansas, came here at his own expense to videotape our SOS outreach and put together a presentation for us. In 1983, we conducted our first Institute of Evangelism.

In 1984, the Democratic Convention came to San Francisco and we planned our summer outreach to coincide with the convention. Thirty churches and ministries joined with us in the outreach and we planned two large Christian rallies in front of the Moscone Center, where the convention was held. Many protest groups had converged on the city that week and were planning large protest rallies. Thousands of media people were here from all over the world. City officials worried about riots and bloodshed. On Thursday, Jerry Falwell spoke at a meeting in San Francisco. A massive demonstration against him resulted in violence and several arrests. On Sunday, there were two marches by the labor unions and gay rights advocates, each with over 100,000 participants. Monday featured a massive anti-war rally with about 60,000 demonstrators outside the Moscone Center. Among them were tens of thousands of punk rockers and "skinheads" who had come here for the convention. Several dozen of them were arrested.

Tuesday afternoon featured a pro-marijuana rally at the Moscone Center. At the same time, a thousand Christians gathered at Union Square and marched through downtown San Francisco to the Moscone Center for a worship rally with Chuck Girard. Many of the punk rockers at the marijuana rally stayed for our rally, and we witnessed to them. As we worshipped the Lord for several hours, the spiritual atmosphere in the rally area changed. The next day we had another worship rally at the Moscone Center with evangelist Mario Murillo. Again, the presence of the Holy Spirit in the area was strong. After our rally, a "Peace in El Salvador rally" was planned. We stayed to witness. Their rally only drew about 200 people. The Christian presence was so strong in the area — with hundreds of Christians preaching, carrying signs, and witnessing — that people would arrive in the area, see all the Christians, and leave, thinking it was a Christian rally!

The next day, the National Organization of Women, one of the most influential groups in the country with over 250,000 members, had planned a rally on the day the first woman was nominated as Vice-President. We sent all our workers there to pray, worship, and witness. Again, their demonstration fizzled with at most 300 demonstrators, all of whom heard about Jesus. During the week, we witnessed to many of the delegates, including Gary Hart and George McGovern.

In January 1985, the Superbowl came to Stanford Stadium. We planned a large outreach in San Francisco and at the stadium in Palo Alto. Evangelist James Robison joined us for this outreach. He preached in downtown San Francisco and at the

Superbowl. His TV crew filmed the outreach and put together two shows that went on national television, informing a million Christians about the evangelistic work in San Francisco. In July 1985, several Christian ministries in southern California held the first annual SOS-Hollywood outreach, a city-wide outreach to that city based upon SOS-San Francisco. In August 1985, our sixth annual SOS-San Francisco outreach featured a march through downtown San Francisco and a baptism of thirty-one people in the fountain in front of City Hall.

Also in 1985, we began working with evangelist Jerry Brandt, who works with singles ministries throughout Northern California and hosts a program on Christian TV in the San Francisco area. Jerry got his singles groups involved in feeding the poor at our outreaches. He also began praying for the sick at the outreaches. At our Christmas outreach, he raised the funds to purchase a thousand sleeping bags to give away to the homeless. All three network TV stations featured stories on the outreach and the Sunday newspaper had a large article on it. This outreach was a powerful witness of the love of Christ to the people of San Francisco. For too long, non-Christian groups have been helping the poor while Christians have been doing very little. This was an opportunity to demonstrate Christ's love by helping people with their physical — as well as their spiritual — needs.

15 _____

Organizing a City-wide Evangelistic Outreach

When evangelist Luis Palau came to San Francisco in 1980, he gave five reasons for having a mass evangelistic crusade:

1. The gospel goes to many thousands more people than if just one or two churches were involved.

2. The whole city becomes "God-conscious" for the period of the outreach, making Jesus Christ and the Bible common topics of discussion among all groups of people for much longer.

3. The powers of darkness are disrupted as the light of Christ is firmly held up by a united church.

4. As a result of this disruption of Satan's strongholds, evangelism becomes easier.

5. Churches grow and plant new churches in areas of the city where crusade decisions reveal a need.

Once your street witnessing team has been going for a while, you may want to plan a large, city-wide outreach in your community. One way to do this is to plan it around a special event. Almost every city has at least one special event each year — such as a big parade or festival. During this time, there will be a lot of extra people to witness to. Also, it is easier to get Christians excited about witnessing at a special event.

You will need to start planning several months before the outreach. For the outreach to be successful, one or more people need to commit themselves to work very hard at planning the outreach, making sure every detail is worked out. For the SOS-San Francisco outreach, a steering committee of six leaders meets about five times a year to provide basic direction for the outreach. I spend much of the year working out many of the details. During the first year, everything was new and I needed a lot of outside help. Now, many of the details are routine — putting together publicity literature, sending out public service announcements to the radio stations, writing newsletters, arranging housing for workers, getting loudspeaker permits and bands, meeting with pastors, youth leaders and other such things.

How do you get churches involved in your outreach? You can start by visiting some of the key pastors in your community. Call the church office and set up an appointment with the pastor. If someone from that church is already involved in street witnessing, bring him with you. Dress neatly. Share about the street witnessing team, your desire to see more Christians involved in evangelism in the community and to see various churches working together, and about the city-wide outreach. Ask him what he thinks could be done to get the people in his church involved.

Perhaps you could speak at his church — to the entire congregation, to a discipleship class or a youth group. You could take some pictures of your street witnessing and put together a simple slide show. Ask him if he would attend one or two planning meetings before the outreach, and if he would really encourage people in his church to get involved in the outreach. Invite his church to help with follow-up. *Take Him to the Streets* has an excellent chapter (#89) on "Working with and Visiting Churches."

It is also a good idea to meet with youth pastors of the key churches in your area. If a youth pastor is supportive of your ministry, he can get his entire youth group involved. Most youth leaders really want their young people to get serious with the Lord. Street witnessing can help young people see the challenge God has given them to reach others. If we can get Christians to start witnessing when they are young, they will develop a pattern that is likely to continue as they grow older.

Most people who receive Christ do so before they are 18. In general, young people are most effective with people their own age, as they relate better. Also, they have natural contacts with unsaved friends in the public schools. Unfortunately, most teenage Christians do not witness to their unsaved friends because of peer pressure. Often, it is easier for them to start witnessing to strangers on the street. As they grow in boldness, they will find it easier to witness to their friends. A high school student who is committed to the Lord and not afraid to witness can be used to bring many others to Christ. A high school youth group that is committed to Christ can turn its schools upside down. Ask the youth pastor if you can speak with his group about street witnessing. We have had a number of high school groups involved in our outreaches in San Francisco. They are very effective on the streets. Street witnessing really helps them get excited about serving God.

Once you have met some pastors and youth pastors, you can form an outreach planning committee. Invite pastors and other mature Christian leaders in your community who are supportive of your work to join the committee. Schedule three or four planning meetings, 4-6 weeks apart, before the outreach. Explain to them that you don't want token participation, but that you expect them to participate in planning the outreach, and to get their churches involved. Put together an agenda before the meeting, and give out copies to each participant. Some of the items you will need to discuss include: *Publicity* — printing up posters and other literature, getting other churches involved. *Literature* — printing up tracts, purchasing Bibles. *Finance* — putting together a budget for the outreach. Ask each church to make a commitment toward the budget. *Evangelistic methods* — At a parade, you may want to make a Christian float. At a fair, you could get a booth. You could print up a special newspaper for the event. You could have one or more concerts or worship rallies. Ask for ideas. *Training* — you could do a special institute before the outreach to train people to witness on the streets. *Recruiting workers from the churches for evangelism and follow-up* — you could offer to speak about the outreach in various churches.

Ask for input from the pastors as you discuss each item. Delegate as much work as you can. Perhaps one church will print up the tracts. Another will purchase Bibles. Another will make a float, or some signs, or will design and print a poster. If you delegate work, make sure it actually gets done. Ask the pastors to speak about the outreach with other pastors they know, and encourage them to get involved.

At the end of each meeting, schedule a time for the next meeting. After the meeting, write each pastor to remind him about the next meeting. You can include a summary of what happened at the last meeting, what each person committed himself to do, and what will be discussed at the next meeting.

Publicizing the Outreach

Generally, it takes a lot of publicity to get Christians involved in an evangelistic outreach. We normally start by printing up literature — posters, fliers, information sheets, inserts for church bulletins. The literature should give information about the outreach — what you will be doing, when and where you will meet, who to contact for more information plus your address and phone number.

Then, we distribute this literature to churches, Christian bookstores, and Christian schools. Also, we have put together a mailing list of people who have shown an interest in our ministry, and we send out a regular newsletter to them. Many of these people help us publicize the outreach by putting up posters, talking to pastors, giving out fliers, etc.

We go to major Christian events in our area, such as concerts, to distribute literature. The promoter of the local Christian concerts lets us set up a booth at many of his concerts, through which we reach many Christians. Most Christian radio and TV stations have talk shows where they interview various Christian leaders, and they will probably want to have you on the show. This will help you to reach a lot of Christians in your community. Call the station and talk with the station manager or program manager about this.

Christian Concerts and Worship Rallies

We have found in San Francisco that concerts and worship rallies are an effective way of getting Christians involved in evangelism and of drawing in unbelievers to hear the gospel. You may want to plan one or more concerts or rallies for your city-wide outreach. First, choose a location. In San Francisco, we found that it is very difficult to get unbelievers into a church or meeting hall. Instead we plan concerts and rallies in outdoor parks which already have a lot of people in them, so we don't have to draw a crowd. If you decide to do an outdoor event, pick a location and time when there will be a lot of people around. Call the police department to find out how you go about getting a permit for the area. You may want to reserve several different times, or try a few different locations.

Next, find a music group. Ask Christians you know about various local Christian groups. Most will play for free, or for travel expenses. If possible, listen to a tape of the group before you decide to use them. Look for a group that is reasonably good musically and, more important, wants to minister to the lost.

Worship rallies are often more effective than outdoor concerts in reaching people. When a group of Christians gathers together to worship the Lord, the presence of the Holy Spirit is felt by everyone who comes near the area. Many people are drawn to Christ in such an atmosphere. While the worship group you use should be proficient musically, it is more important that they be able to lead Christians into true worship, into the presence of God.

Conducting an Institute of Evangelism

You may want to organize an evangelism training institute before your outreach. The institute will help train workers in evangelism, and help them to get excited about witnessing and feel more confident about their ability to witness. We normally schedule our institute all day Friday and Saturday a few weeks before our major outreach. The institute should include some practical teachings in how to witness, some small group sessions where people can ask questions, and a final message to encourage people to come to the outreach and get others involved.

Attending an evangelism institute is much less threatening than witnessing. You may be able to attract a lot of Christians who have never witnessed on the streets before, including whole youth groups, if you print up some fliers and publicize the institute well. If you make witnessing seem complicated, you will scare people off. Let them know that what they learn at the institute won't do any good unless they use it, and that they will have an opportunity to apply what they have learned at the outreach. We have found that many of those who come to our institute will also join us for the outreach.

Outreach Logistics

Many details are involved in planning an outreach. You need to put together a schedule and find a central meeting place. Normally, we meet in a church. The first day, we have an orientation meeting in which we explain what will be going on during the outreach, how we expect workers to behave on the streets, and some basic witnessing instructions. We also introduce workers to the outreach leaders, go over the schedule, and answer questions. Before each witnessing time, we meet at the church for a time of worship and prayer, a short inspirational message or some testimonies, and some brief instructions.

When people arrive for the outreach, they are asked to fill out a registration form. They are given a schedule of activities for the week and a policy statement which explains our position on various issues that might come up. We also give them a list of names, addresses, phone numbers, and meeting times of churches involved in follow-up. Another flier, called a "survival sheet," has referral information for people who need a place to stay, or free food, medical help, employment advice, and welfare information.

When people register for an outreach, we assign them to a

team. Each team consists of a leader and about twenty workers. The leader needs to be a mature Christian with witnessing experience. The leader's job is to pastor his team, to help them with their witnessing, and to take care of any problems that may arise. The key to a successful outreach is having good team leaders. If a group comes from a single church and wants to stay together, we put them on one team. They can use their own leader, if they have one.

One of your outreach leaders will need to oversee the team leaders. He should meet with them daily and take care of any problems that arise. Also, he will need to work out the locations where each team will go each day.

If workers will be coming in from out of town, you need to arrange housing for them. One way to do this is to find a single church (or two) where they can stay. If possible, arrange for some people to cook meals for them. Other possibilities are to house people in a college dorm or in homes of local Christians. Showers could be a problem. Is there a public shower facility at a swimming pool or a school you could use? Transporting workers is another problem. Can you borrow some vans or buses? Often there are enough cars to transport everyone.

At the end of each church meeting, we usually take an offering to cover the expenses of the outreach. Each year we go into debt several thousand dollars as we print up publicity literature, tracts, and incur other expenses. By the end of each outreach we have always received enough in the offerings to pay our bills.

When the church meeting is dismissed, we make sure every person is assigned to a team, and have the workers meet with their team leader for prayer and instructions for the day. As they leave the church, they pick up tracts and literature on the tables outside the sanctuary. You can write your own tracts or get some from a tract company. Some tract companies will send you tracts for free or for whatever you can donate. *Take Him to the Streets* has a list of addresses for tract companies. Make sure you stamp all tracts with a local address and phone number where people can get help.

If there are people in your community who speak a foreign

language, you should have tracts in these languages. Also, you should have tracts written for children. Each worker should take a list of addresses and meeting times of local churches and follow-up cards, on which they write the name, address, phone number and other pertinent information of people who pray to receive Christ.

Follow-up

We have found that personal contact is the key to follow-up. When you meet someone on the street and he responds to what you say, you have developed a rapport with him that will greatly help in follow-up. It is best if you can visit him, or at least call or write him, yourself. If you are from out of town, try to introduce him to a local Christian when you first meet him on the street, so he can do the follow-up. We need to take a genuine interest in the people we talk with, especially new believers. If a local Christian can develop a friendship with a new believer, he can help that person get established in his church, and in the Lord.

Try to make your initial follow-up visit within 24 hours after the person prays to receive Christ. Otherwise, Satan may attack the new believer, tell him what he did wasn't real, and persuade him to return to his old ways. If we encourage people to count the cost before praying to receive Christ and clearly explain the gospel, we will see more genuine conversions.

Some new believers will not grow in the Lord unless they can get into some kind of Christian living situation. This is especially true in large cities such as San Francisco, where there are many people with life-controlling problems such as drug addiction, alcoholism, sexual perversion, and mental disturbances. Some of these people can be referred to Christian programs such as Teen Challenge. *The National Street Ministry Directory*, available at Box P-1, Felton, CA 95018, has a list of Christian live-in houses and programs. There may be Christian families or singles who want to take someone into their home. Also, you may consider starting your own live-in discipleship house.

After each witnessing session, we have the workers give the

follow-up cards they have filled out to their team leader, who gives them to the outreach leader in charge of follow-up. Each local church that is involved in follow-up will have their own visitation team. The cards will be distributed to the various churches.

After the outreach is over, we send one or two letters to each new believer, encouraging him in his spiritual growth and offering help and counseling. If you include a response sheet and a return envelope, many will respond to the letter. Items we use on the response sheet include: I would like someone to visit me; I would like a Bible study course sent to my home; I need a New Testament; Please pray for me about these needs: ——————— ; Other: ——————— .

Finance

Our ministry sends out a monthly newsletter that relates what is happening in our ministry, announces upcoming outreaches, sometimes contains a brief teaching on evangelism, and presents our needs. We try to make our needs known in a straightforward manner. Often, we have seen God meet needs that we never told anyone about. While God usually provides our needs through His people, He wants us to depend on Him, not on people. We also take offerings at meetings composed primarily of Christians, but we don't take offerings at evangelistic meetings.

The Christian world has been inundated by all kinds of financial appeals. I receive mailings from about a hundred ministries. Some are honest in their request for finances, but many use various gimmicks to manipulate people to give to their ministry. Some pastors and evangelists use similarly dishonest methods to get large offerings at churches. These methods do generate large amounts of money, which is why so many ministries use them. However, such methods are dishonoring to God and a stumblingblock to unbelievers, who laugh at the greed and hypocrisy.

Communicating a Vision

During the institute of evangelism and church meetings at the outreach, you will have some opportunities to share your vision for ministry with the Christians who attend. Take advantage of these meetings to stir up the saints to continue to witness boldly for Christ, to change their community and world. Suggest ministry opportunities they can get involved with. Each of us is important in God's plan. We need to be obedient to His calling in our lives.

For too long, Christians have been sitting around, waiting for Jesus to return. We need to see that we have a mission to fulfill on this earth, that Jesus has called us to take the gospel to the people in our community and to the whole world. We have been drafted into God's army, but most of us are A.W.O.L. (absent without leave). We need to get back on the front lines.

A packet of forms we use in SOS-San Francisco is available free upon request. The following forms are included in the packet: Public service announcement, follow-up information and sample follow-up letter, SOS registration form, SOS policy statement, and SOS information sheets. Also included is a street meeting check list designed by Mike Zello of Washington D.C. Teen Challenge. You may receive this packet by mailing us the Reader Response Sheet in the back of this book.

16

Starting a Discipleship House Ministry

After you have been involved in street ministry for a while, you will meet many people who pray to receive Christ, but find it difficult or impossible to grow spiritually in their present living situation. Some people have no regular living situation, and survive by begging, stealing, selling drugs or prostituting. Some people live with a male or female lover, or have room-mates who are involved in drugs or sexual immorality. Many new believers will not grow spiritually unless they can get into a Christian living situation immediately after they are saved.

Unfortunately, it is not always easy to find a good Christian living situation for a new believer. The *National Street Ministry Directory* has listings of Christian live-in houses around the country. Get acquainted with the houses in your area. The best way to do this is to visit them. Find out as much as you can about a program before sending someone there. If possible, talk to some people who have been through the program, or are in it right now.

While all live-in programs need rules, some are excessively strict and manipulative. Avoid programs that expect people to stay indefinitely. The purpose of a live-in program should be to help a person grow spiritually so that he will eventually be able to live a Christian life without such support.

Also, a program may be able to help only certain kinds of people. Many programs are very successful with drug addicts but not with homosexuals. Make sure the new believer understands what is involved in entering a program, such as the rules and the time commitment, before he enters.

In San Francisco, we have sent dozens of people to various discipleship programs. Most left within a few days. Very few stayed longer than three months at any of the programs. Some people could not adapt to the rules. Others had trouble making friends in the new situation, or didn't feel much love. Others were drawn away by the temptation to return to their old ways.

Over the years, it became increasingly clear to us that we needed to start our own discipleship house ministry. We had put so much time and energy seeking to bring people to Christ. It was very frustrating to see so many fall away because we could not find a good Christian living situation for them.

We realized we would have two major problems: obtaining finances and finding the right house leader. We wanted the house leader to be supported financially so he could dedicate himself fully to ministering to the new believers.

In order to run a successful discipleship house, you need to have the right leader. The house leader needs to be a mature Christian who can lead and at the same time be a servant. He needs to set a good example for the other house members. He needs to know when to be gentle and patient with people, and when to be firm. The position is a very demanding one, since people will constantly be coming to him with problems. You should also have an assistant leader who can oversee the house so the leader can take at least one day off each week.

Our first discipleship house was established in 1984. We had written about the need for a house for several months in our newsletter and raised about $350 in monthly support. We had hoped to raise about $1000 monthly but we decided to go ahead with the house. Ron Woodruff, my co-worker in SOS Ministries, agreed to be the house leader until we could find someone else. We rented a house and it was soon filled with new believers. Initially we required that everyone in the house get a job. However, many of the people who moved in were not able to get or hold a job so we allowed them to stay on welfare temporarily.

In California there are two kinds of welfare: general assistance and social security (SSI). The general assistance required that people actively look for work, so it wasn't a problem for us. However, some of our people were on SSI, which gave them an assured check as long as they could prove to their social worker that they were incapable of working. This was a real problem, as these people were forced to convince themselves and others that they couldn't work. We found that they would grow very little spiritually until they were willing to get off SSI. Most found it very hard to give up that guaranteed monthly income.

The house functioned fairly well as long as Ron was the leader. However, after about six months Ron got married and left the house. We were unable to find a good leader so we closed the house.

We continued to pray for a house and in the summer of 1985, a married couple, Wes and Paula Dennison, wrote us that they were interested in leading a house. About the same time, we met a man who owned a house he was willing to let us use rent free. So we started a new house. In this house, the new believers spend four hours daily in Bible study and prayer and four hours working. One staff member leads a work crew. We are hoping to establish a business to allow the house members to work together. This house has been very successful, largely because of the emphasis by the house leaders on prayer and fasting. Most of the new believers who moved into the house have stayed, and are growing steadily in the Lord.

Training Christian Families to Disciple New Believers

Discipleship houses are very expensive to operate and good house leaders are hard to find. Leading a discipleship house requires great spiritual maturity and willingness to work long hours for little or no pay. The demand for such houses always greatly exceeds the supply. Our discipleship house filled up as soon as it opened, and it has remained full.

Many of the new believers we encounter in street ministry can best be helped in a Christian family or household of single people. For example, many of the teenagers we meet on the street have never had a good family life and have lived in institutions all their life. They really need a Christian family to take them in and love them.

Setting up a program like this involves the following four steps:

1. Recruiting families (and households of single people). We need to let Christians know of this need and how they can help. Christians need to be reminded of their responsibility to help others in the Body of Christ. The Bible says much about our responsibility to show hospitality, especially to other believers, and to help people with their needs, not just say, ''Be warmed and filled.''

Some parents are concerned that these new believers may be a bad influence on their children. Actually, they should be a very good influence. If parents can show their children that their Christian faith is genuine, as demonstrated by this act of Christian love, their children are more likely to follow Christ. Also, the zeal of the new convert can help the children get excited about serving God. The children can see the life-changing power of Jesus Christ in this person's life. Too many Christian parents live selfish, worldly lives and wonder why their children turn away from God.

2. Training. We need to offer training for Christians who want to take in new believers. We need to prepare them for problems they may have. For example, many Christians are concerned about someone stealing from them. First, we need to commit our possessions to God and be more concerned about people than things. Second, we need to take reasonable precautions to avoid stealing. One way is to make a rule that the person cannot stay at home when there is no other adult present. The new believer should be kept busy either going to school or looking for work.

3. Screening and matching. We must screen new believers so that, as much as possible, only those who are serious about following Christ are put in homes. We need to screen out as many con artists and thieves as we can. Also, we should learn enough about the new Christians and the families to enable them to be properly matched.

4. Support. We need to help the families and new believers make the necessary adjustments to living together. There are many problems involved, and not every match will be successful, at least in the short run.

Eight years ago, I lived in a house with four other Christians. We took in a young man who told us a dramatic story of his conversion. All of us believed him, until one day I found out that his story was a lie. I confronted him with it and he left. Several years later I met him. He apologized to me for lying and told me that God used that situation to confront him with his sin and bring him to a genuine repentance.

Christian families offer a tremendous untapped resource for helping the many hundreds of new believers who need to get into a Christian environment in order to grow in Christ. Despite the obstacles, it is the only way we will be able to meet this great need. We must start recruiting and training Christians to open their homes to new believers.

17

Recruiting and Training Leaders

If you want your ministry to grow, you need leaders who can take on much of the responsibilities, so that you don't have to do all the work yourself. Also, a good leader will have gifts and insights to take your ministry in directions you could never have seen. Where do you get these leaders?

In our ministry, God directed us to start a house for potential ministry leaders. We advertised in our newsletter and spoke with the people who went out on the streets with us about the house, and it was soon filled. At first, we weren't very careful about who we let move into the house. Some weren't very strong Christians; others didn't have the same vision for evangelism that we had. Also, we didn't have a very good idea of what to do with these people once they joined us.

After several years, we started being more selective in choosing house members. We began looking for spiritual maturity, willingness to serve, and desire to be involved in this ministry. We started teaching our house members about leadership, and giving them opportunities to lead. Every Tuesday night, we have a leadership training meeting. Some weeks we teach about qualities of a leader, such as being a servant. Other weeks we have guest speakers or videotaped teachings.

We also give each of our trainees an opportunity to lead a witnessing team. This involves giving instructions to the workers before they go out, and in watching over the team on the streets. The team leader needs to make sure new witnessers are paired up with someone with experience, and to help with any problems they have on the streets. Often, Christians who are witnessing on the streets for the first time will have a frightening experience. Someone may threaten to hurt them, or tell them they are being unloving. They may find that nobody will want to talk with them, or may have trouble starting a conversation. They may have a hard time accepting the methods that we use on the streets, such as preaching or carrying signs. The leader needs to watch for these things, and minister to the needs of his workers. Otherwise, many of the new workers will not return.

Meanwhile, we are looking for new people who can be trained as leaders for discipleship houses and other areas of ministry. We share about this need in our newsletter and at our evangelism outreaches. When we speak at churches and youth groups, we talk about this need. We have filled out an application with Intercristo, which is a computerized job placement agency for Christians. (Their address is Box 33487, Seattle, WA 98133.) Also, we've sent letters out to other ministry leaders, letting them know of our needs. Christian schools and ministries with training programs such as Youth With a Mission (Box 4600, Tyler, TX 75712) are good sources for potential leaders.

Our main source for leaders, however, has been the people who have witnessed on the streets with us. As our ministry grows, we expect that some of the people we have led to Christ on the streets, and helped in our discipleship houses, will ultimately become leaders in this ministry. As we contact other ministries for potential leaders, most of them also need more leaders. If we want more leaders, it seems, we will need to train them ourselves.

Characteristics of a Good Leader

In this section, I'd like to describe some of the qualities we are looking for in recruiting people to train as leaders, and also the qualities we would like to impart to potential leaders:

1. Willing to serve. Jesus said, "He that is greatest among you shall be your servant" (Matt. 23:11). Jesus Himself set our example by washing His disciples' feet. We need, first, a desire to serve God. As we give ourselves to Him, He will give us a love for His people and a desire to serve them.

2. Diligence. "He that is faithful in that which is least is faithful also in much" (Luke 16:10). God will raise up into leadership those who are faithful in the small things He gives them to do. "Promotion comes neither from the east, nor from the west . . . but God is the judge: he puts down one, and sets another up" (Psalm 75:6-7). Sometimes people complain that they are not being raised up into leadership quickly enough. If you are faithful in the things God has set before you, He will place you in leadership in His time. When God opens the door for you to be a leader, no man can stand in your way.

3. Brokenness. "Every branch that bears fruit, he purges it, that it may bring forth more fruit" (John 15:2). "Whosoever shall fall on that stone (Christ) shall be broken" (Luke 20:18). "The sacrifices of God are a broken spirit: a broken and a contrite heart, O God, you will not despise" (Psalm 51:17). When Jesus told Peter he would deny Him, Peter insisted that he wouldn't. After he denied Christ three times, Peter was broken. He knew he couldn't rely on his own strength. He needed to rely on the Lord. Paul wrote that a bishop should not be a new believer, "lest being lifted up with pride he fall into the condemnation of the devil" (1 Tim. 3:6). God needs to break each of us of our pride. Sometimes a new believer will have natural leadership abilities, and we will put him in leadership too soon. This can be very destructive both to him and those he leads. "The trying of your faith works patience. But let patience have her perfect work, that you may be perfect and complete, lacking in nothing" (James 1:3,4). Christian maturity comes only through enduring trials. "But we had the sentence of death in ourselves, that we should not trust in ourselves, but in God who raises the dead" (2 Cor. 1:9). Those are the words of a broken man.

4. Able to exercise authority. There are times when a decision must be made and action must be taken. For example, a house leader must remove someone from his house who consistently refuses to obey house rules. He must be confident of the authority God has given him as leader, but not abuse that authority. "Feed the flock of God . . . . Not being lords over God's people, but being examples to the flock" (1 Peter 5:2-3).

A good leader will see a need and meet it — either by doing it himself or delegating it to someone else, and making sure it gets done. He needs to give responsibilities to others, so they can become leaders and he will not be overly burdened. But he also needs to remain a servant.

In order to exercise authority, a leader must be submitted to authority. "Where no counsel is, the people fall: but in the multitude of counselors there is safety" (Prov. 11:14). Any ministry or house needs a governing board of mature Christians that a leader can look to for counsel. SOS Ministries has a steering committee of six pastors and ministry leaders. This committee meets five times a year, and I consult them about all major decisions.

5. Other qualities. A good leader needs a good relationship with God. He needs to maintain a good prayer life. This is difficult when he is busy with responsibilities, but essential. He needs to pray for ministry needs and those he is working with. He needs to walk by faith. He must be able to discern the will of God in various situations. "Not by might, nor by power, but by my Spirit, says the Lord" (Zech. 4:6).

A good leader needs to be a giver. He needs to give his time, his money, his whole self into the work of the ministry. As Jesus' disciple, he must deny himself, pick up his cross, and follow his Lord. Ministry work generally involves great personal sacrifice — long hours, working for little or no pay, receiving little appreciation and much criticism from others. However, at times we must rest, take a day off to relax, spend some time alone with the Lord. A married leader needs to make sure he does not neglect his family.

Finally, a good leader needs to be sensitive to people. He should spend time getting to know and caring for those he works with. He needs to be a good counselor. He must think before he talks, so he doesn't offend others with careless words. "A brother offended is harder to be won than a strong city" (Prov. 18:19).

18 ⸻

Personal Discipleship in the Life of a Street Minister

1. Prayer and God's Word

Any person who is involved in ministry for the Lord needs to be careful not to neglect the One he is ministering for. In the second chapter of Revelation, the church of Ephesus was full of good works, but they had left their first love. It is easy to become like Martha, who was busy working for Jesus, rather than Mary, who sat at His feet and listened to Him.

In John 15, Jesus says that it is impossible for us to bear fruit unless we abide in Him. In Acts 4, after the chief priests had questioned Peter and John about the healing of the lame man, it says that when they saw their boldness, "and perceived that they were unlearned and ignorant men, they marvelled; and they took knowledge of them, that they had been with Jesus." When people look at our lives, can they tell that we have been with Jesus?

In Acts 6, the church appointed deacons to look over the treatment of widows so that the apostles could give themselves "continually to prayer, and to the ministry of the Word." It is easy for us to get so involved in the details of ministry that we neglect what is most important, the time we spend with our Lord, in prayer and in the Word. We need to receive fresh direction from Him, and a fresh anointing, so that we do not get into a rut and miss out on what He has for us. We can easily become like Peter who had toiled all night at fishing and had caught nothing. Jesus told him to cast his net on the other side and it got so full he could hardly bring it in.

Many who are involved in God's work have become victims of ministry burnout. Let me give my view of why this happens. After we have been involved in ministry for a while, we may find ourselves doing ministry work our own way and in our own strength, not God's way, in His strength. We can easily lose the joy and excitement that comes out of a daily walk with Christ, and our ministry work can become burdensome. Jesus said His yoke is easy and His burden is light. God gives us abundant grace to do the work He has called us to do, but often we get involved in activities that God has not told us to do.

Ask God to search your heart, to soften it so it will be sensitive to hear and obey Him, and to show you areas of your life where you are resisting His Spirit and blocking fellowship with Him. Any ministry we do needs to be the natural expression of our relationship with Jesus Christ. The experience we had with Him when we were saved will not sustain us through our Christian walk; it needs to be renewed each day. Our chief source of joy and fulfillment needs to come from that relationship, not from our ministry work. If it doesn't, you are a candidate for ministry burnout. Take this advice seriously. For some of you, this could be the most important message in this book.

2. Personal Holiness

We live in perilous times. Many ministers are getting involved in sexual immorality: adultery, fornication, homosexuality, and even child molestation. As a result, their ministries are destroyed, many believers are stumbled and Christianity is discredited in the eyes of the world. Many ministers neglect their wives and families in their dedication to the ministry, and end up getting divorced.

Other ministries have been destroyed through improper handling of finances. Sometimes this involves theft and embezzlement of ministry funds. In other cases, it is more a matter of deception — dishonest fund-raising tactics or unwise use of funds. Or it could be a matter of being careless in handling funds — spending excessively and getting heavily in debt — or poor bookkeeping.

Paul said, "I keep under my body, and bring it into subjection: lest by any means, when I have preached to others, I myself should be a castaway" (1 Cor. 9:27). We need to know our own limitations. "Let him who thinks he stands take heed lest he fall" (1 Cor. 10:12).

Also, we need to maintain a relationship with other mature Christians to whom we can go for counsel. As we get into a place of leadership, it is harder for us to admit our weaknesses to others. Christians expect us to "have it together" and it is often easier not to admit our weaknesses. It is not necessary to admit all our shortcomings or sins to everyone, but we need to find mature Christians with whom we can share these things. "In the multitude of counselors there is safety" (Prov. 11:14). "Confess your faults one to another, and pray for one another, that you may be healed" (James 5:16).

If we do not deal with little sins in our life, they tend to grow into bigger sins. They may not totally destroy our ministry, but they can hinder our effectiveness. They can hinder our prayer life, our ability to hear from God, and our joy in the Lord. If we are not being honest with ourselves, it will reflect in our ministry and hinder our ability to draw Christians and unbelievers closer to Christ. We should pray with the psalmist, "Search me, O God, and know my heart: try me, and know my thoughts: and see if there be any wicked way in me, and lead me in the way everlasting" (Psalm 139:23-24).

Every Christian, I suppose, has lustful thoughts. If we dwell on these thoughts, they can easily lead to immoral activities such as pornography or fornication. Trying to fight the thoughts doesn't work. We need to fill our mind with pure thoughts.

As much as possible, we should avoid situations that encourage lustful thoughts. Some of the streets I witness on would be a real problem for me were I to spend a lot of time on them for no particular purpose. But I only go on these streets to witness and while I am there my mind is centered on Christ and bringing the lost to Him. New believers often need to stay away from certain neighborhoods, even for witnessing.

3. Handling Finances

Jesus said, "If you have not been faithful in the unrighteous mammon, who will commit to your trust the true riches?" (Luke 16:11). I believe that all the money we have (not just ten percent) is entrusted to us by God to use for His service. God will hold us accountable for what we do with what He has given us. When people donate funds to our ministry, we have a responsibility to them as well as to God to use the funds wisely, to the best of our ability. We need to keep good records of how we spend ministry funds, and to avoid extravagance and unnecessary expenses. We should also avoid large debts, except where God is clearly directing us to do things. In these situations, we should seek out godly counsel. Your ministry needs to have an advisory board of godly men from whom you can receive this counsel. A regular financial report for the ministry should be made to this board. The board should be consulted about all major expenses.

In terms of personal finances, I believe that God would have us simplify our lifestyle. We are surrounded by advertising and other influences to persuade us to buy things we don't really need. We don't necessarily need to wear the latest fashions or drive a new car. Sometimes, Christians say that they need these things to be able to witness to wealthy people. But Jesus and Paul didn't need to be rich to witness to kings and rich people. Some of us could save a lot of money by living with other Christians. Cutting down on our living expenses can leave more money to give to God's work. It also can free us to give more of our time to God's work. Many single persons could work part time and give the rest of their time to ministry work, if they would cut down on their expenses. We should be very careful about going into debt; it brings us into bondage as we are forced to work more, and have less time and money for God's work.

"Godliness with contentment is great gain. For we brought nothing into this world, and it is certain that we can carry nothing out. And having food and clothing let us be content. But they that will be rich fall into temptation and a snare, and into many foolish and hurtful lusts that plunge men into ruin and destruction. For the love of money is the root of all evil: which while some coveted after, they have erred from the faith, and pierced themselves through with many sorrows'' (1 Tim. 6:6-10).

4. Rest

After six days of work, God rested on the seventh day. I believe that we need to take time to be alone with the Lord, and also to take time just to relax and get away from our work. I personally like to take a day every week, whenever possible, and take a walk in the country. By the end of the day I am relaxed and can return to my work with a fresh perspective.

I believe that we should work hard for the Lord, but we should also know when to rest. When I have been under a lot of pressure, I find that time of rest is especially important. Every year, after our big summer outreach, I take a week to get away and relax. This is also a time when I can think about what I have been doing, and seek God's direction for the next year.

19 ⸻

Pastors and Evangelists Join Together

In recent years, I have observed three changes in the church in the United States that really encourage me. First, *a healing is taking place between the pastor and the evangelist.* Due to the nature of their gifts, pastors are concerned about caring for their flocks, while evangelists are concerned about reaching out to the lost. Unfortunately, these interests have been seen as competing. Many pastors feel threatened by the evangelist, who seeks to get Christians involved in outreach. The pastor is concerned that his flock is not ready to be involved in ministry, that they first need to be taught more of God's Word and counseled with personal problems. He is concerned about follow-up of new believers from evangelistic outreaches. He is also concerned that traveling evangelists will steal people from his church and divert their finances from the church. He may believe that ministry should come out of the local church rather than ''parachurch'' ministries.

The evangelist, on the other hand, is often critical of the complacency he sees in the local church and its lack of evangelistic activity. He has probably experienced a lot of rejection from local churches as he has tried to get people involved in evangelism and been criticized by pastors for his activity. He may have pretty much given up on the local church and come to believe that God will move outside it. So he starts his own ministry or works as an independent evangelist. He may go to churches to raise funds, but otherwise he has no interest in the local church.

Fortunately, a change is beginning to take place in this unhealthy situation. Pastors and evangelists are beginning to see that they need each other. Ephesians 4 says that God gave us apostles, prophets and teachers "for the perfecting of the saints unto the work of the ministry, for the building up of the body of Christ." The function of the pastor is to equip the church to do the work of ministry, not to try to do it all himself. The task of the evangelist is not to do all the evangelizing himself but to train and motivate the church to witness. A church that does not reach out to the lost is not healthy, regardless of how good their Bible teaching is. The church needs the evangelist to be doing his job in it.

In SOS Ministries, we see our function as serving the local church. We want to train Christians in evangelism. We want to see local churches start their own outreach ministries. We refer those who come to Christ during our outreaches to local churches for follow-up. We also believe that God would have churches cooperate with one another.

The second change I have noticed is that *churches are starting to work together*. In John 17, Jesus prayed that his church would be one "that the world may know that you have sent me." Too often, unbelievers have only seen the division and conflict between churches, and this has kept many people from Christ. We have seen that evangelistic outreaches have been very effective in bringing churches of various denominations together. One thing that all evangelical churches can agree on is that we need to preach the gospel. When we are on the front lines witnessing for the Lord, we are not thinking about what's wrong with each other's doctrine.

When I first came to San Francisco, there seemed to be little relationship between churches. When we first started doing evangelistic outreaches, we received a lot of criticism, but little support, from the local churches. During our second year, God showed us to reach out to the local churches and serve them, helping them do outreaches in their own neighborhood centered around their own churches. About twenty churches responded. I believe that the relationship between us and the various local churches in the San Francisco Bay Area has been steadily improving. At the same time, we have seen an increasing cooperation between churches. The local National Association of Evangelicals has started a "family reunion" time which draws several hundred Christians from various churches. Christians from different churches have also joined together to establish a Crisis Pregnancy Center and to make a stand on the abortion issue. While change is often slow, pastors are getting to know and trust one another, and to speak well of other churches and their leaders.

The third change I have observed is that *evangelistic ministries throughout the United States are starting to work together.* Evangelists tend to be independent and strong-willed. In the past, most who started their own ministries had little relationship with other evangelists, preferring to "do their own thing." However, God is raising up a new breed of evangelists who desire to serve the local church and to help one another.

For many years, evangelistic ministries have been joining together for an outreach in New Orleans during the Mardi Gras. Out of this, several ministry leaders got to know one another. In the summer of 1984, seven of these leaders joined their skills and finances to plan the first National Street Ministries Conference in Dallas. Over five hundred people registered for this conference. Over fifty different street ministries were represented.

One of the leaders who planned this conference is Jonathan Gainsbrugh. He founded a ministry called Worldshakers for Christ in Tulsa, Oklahoma (now in Santa Cruz, California) and wrote *Take Him to the Streets.* He also has compiled the *National Street Ministry Directory,* a listing of over a thousand street ministries, coffeehouses, live-in discipleship programs, and street preachers. While putting together this directory, he got to know many ministry leaders. When the Directory was published, many of us in evangelistic ministry started to realize that there were many others who were doing street ministry in other places. When we came to the National Street Ministries Conference, we met many of these ministry leaders. As we attended the various workshops, we realized that each of us had learned many things that other ministries, especially those just starting, could benefit from.

Another vision of Jonathan's was to establish the International Street Ministries Association (ISMA). It would provide a means for those who are involved in street ministry to help one another, to provide support for new ministries, and to promote street evangelism in the local church.

After I attended the convention in Dallas, I felt that God wanted me to develop more relationships with others involved in street ministry, to help ISMA get established, and to write this book to share our experiences with others who desire to be involved in street ministry. At this time, ISMA is just beginning to function. Our first efforts are to put out a newsletter, and eventually a magazine, to communicate about street ministry. Also, we are planning regional evangelism conferences to train Christians in street ministry and encourage them to get involved in evangelism. Already, we have conducted two such conferences, one in Northern California and the other in Denver.

As I began writing this book, I sent out a survey to several leaders of evangelistic ministries. I asked them four questions:
1. How did you first get involved in street witnessing?
2. How did your street ministry get started?
3. What is the main vision, emphasis, and future direction for your ministry?
4. What key things has God shown you about starting and operating an effective street ministry?

In the next chapter, I want to share about some of these ministries, and their responses to this survey.

20

What God is Doing in Ten Other Street Ministries

1. The Holy Ghost Repair Service (H.G.R.S.), Box 1590, Hollywood, CA 90078. Judy McPheeters, Director.

Charles McPheeters started the H.G.R.S. in Denver, Colorado in 1971. He was a youth pastor and started taking his people out on the streets so their faith would stay fresh. Later Charles and Judy moved to Hollywood and established a street ministry there. Because of its reputation, young people come to Hollywood from all over the country to make it in show business, or to escape the restrictions at home. They often end up discouraged, broke, and enslaved to drugs, alcohol, and prostitution. For many years, the H.G.R.S. has led street witnessing teams in Hollywood on weekends, as well as witnessing at major outreaches around the country. Starting in 1985, the H.G.R.S., along with Youth With a Mission, began organizing an annual SOS-Hollywood outreach.

In 1982, God took Charles home, and his wife Judy became director of the ministry. But God has been with her and the ministry. Judy's first involvement with street ministry came when she was in college through Campus Crusade for Christ. She met Charles when he came to minister at a coffeehouse operated by Arthur Blessitt.

According to Judy, the main thing in starting and operating an effective street ministry "is to have God's heart of compassion and love for people . . . Also to realize that your ministry is unto the Lord because you can get burnt out very easily when you look at people. Some fall back but we're in it for the long race and not just the short sprint. I've seen people come and go in street ministries but it's those who commit themselves to stay and to serve Jesus in whatever capacity He puts them in who last. Don't be looking for glory or to be a superstar but just to be a servant . . . Stay in a good church. Keep your priorities right. Keep your family in proper priority. They should be more important than the ministry. Keep open communication with the staff and always have a forgiving spirit. Be able to give grace to the people you work with on staff, the way you give grace to the people on the streets. Always be willing to share with someone who has been offended by you or whom you have been offended by and be ready to forgive."

Judy now directs the H.G.R.S. and oversees The Oasis, which is a multi-purpose center. On Friday and Saturday nights, The Oasis has free Christian concerts and is the launching place for the Jesus Night Patrol street witnessing teams. It also features ministry to children at a Kids' Bible Club, a Hope for Hollywood Fellowship meeting on Monday nights, and walk-in counseling and feeding the poor throughout the week.

2. God's Army, Box 4159, Casper, WY 82604. Mike Lockwood, Director.

Mike couldn't find any other Christians in his church who wanted to witness, so he started sharing his vision with the pastors of various churches in his city. By doing church presentations, giving out a ministry brochure to interested people, and word of mouth, a street ministry developed in Casper, Wyoming. Eventually they opened a coffeehouse and Mike went full-time in ministry. Mike's desire is to get a bigger building for their coffeehouse, to work with the International Street Ministries Association (ISMA) to start outreaches in other Wyoming towns, and to take Wyoming people to evangelize at national events.

Asked about the key aspects of operating an effective street ministry, Mike mentioned, "Faithfulness. Having set times to witness and sticking to them. Praise and intercessory prayer. Letting churches know you're not planning to be a church, but want to help them build theirs. Maintaining good relationships with pastors. Letting people know what God is doing through the ministry. Finally, developing key street witnessing people. Make people your priority. Too often I've been bogged down with administrative duties."

3. *Scott Hinkle Outreach Ministries,* Box 380306, Duncan-ville (Dallas area), TX 75138. Scott Hinkle, Director.

Scott started witnessing on the streets as soon as he was saved in 1970. He worked with rehabilitation houses, coffee-houses, as an assistant pastor, and with the Holy Ghost Repair Service, before moving to Dallas. Scott is the main organizer of the National Street Ministries Conference in Dallas. His vision is (1) to see revival in America, (2) for the entire body of Christ to recapture its function as an army and soulwinning organism, and (3) to motivate, mobilize, and activate Christians in reaching their own sphere of influence.

Scott gave six key things God had showed him about operating an effective street ministry:
1. Define your calling and who it is you want to reach — geography, type of person, etc.
2. Stick to what God has called you to do. Accept it, relax, and enjoy it.
3. Don't get stuck in certain types of methods. Be flexible and open to change for the better.
4. Don't let the "needs" of others or yourself run your ministry.
5. Keep your eyes on Jesus.
6. Don't get bitter or allow your heart to become hardened by the needs of those you minister to.

4. *Acts Evangelism,* Box 4314, Missoula, MT 59806. Mike Parrott, Director.

I first met Mike Parrott in 1980, when he was working with Agape, Inc., a street ministry in San Francisco. Almost any day, Mike would be on some street corner preaching with a megaphone. In 1981, Mike went to Missoula, Montana, where he started Acts Evangelism.

The central focus of Acts Evangelism is to equip churches in evangelism. Mike has prepared an extensive three to four day evangelism seminar involving training in many different kinds of evangelism. As part of the seminar, Mike takes the participants witnessing with him. They do street evangelism, campus evangelism, door-to-door witnessing, telephone evangelism, and rock concert evangelism. Mike conducts this seminar primarily in churches in Montana and Washington state, and tries to return to each church every three months. In doing this, Mike hopes to help raise up a strong evangelistic ministry in each church.

Mike places a strong emphasis on intercession. When he goes to a church, he gets the prayer groups in that church praying for the outreach. He also sends out a letter to each member of the church encouraging them to be praying for the outreach and to get involved in a church prayer group. Whenever possible, Mike tries to witness at large events around the country.

Asked about keys to operating an effective street ministry, Mike listed four things:

1. Relationship with Jesus Christ. Deepen your ministry with Jesus and God will prosper your ministry. In order to talk to men successfully about God, we must successfully talk to God about men.

2. Relationship with wife. Stay in agreement and communication with her.

3. Relationship with brethren. Establish relationships with brethren and with the local church and its pastors.

4. Relationship with the lost. Without agape love, I am nothing.

5. *The Hooked on Jesus Ministry*, Box 585, Marietta, GA 33061. Chris Hightower, Director.

One day a man started witnessing to Chris. Chris told him he was saved, so the man gave Chris a handful of tracts and told him to give them out. Chris did, and that's how his street witnessing career began.

After much prayer and a desire to share his vision for the lost with others, Chris contacted the IRS to find out about establishing a non-profit corporation. Then, he started a newsletter and mailed it out to about 250 people. Also, he started writing and printing tracts which he made available to people at whatever they could afford.

Chris takes out street witnessing teams on weekends. During the winter, they also witness door-to-door as people are not out on the streets as much. They take food to the needy as they go to people's homes and help the homeless find food and shelter. They also want to establish closer relationships with local church bodies. In addition, they play music on the streets and at the juvenile hall.

Chris gave six keys to having an effective street ministry:
1. Be absolutely sure you are called to this type of ministry.
2. Keep your personal walk with Christ strong by staying prayed up, filled up, and fired up.
3. Be sure that all your fellow workers are doing the same and that you all have the same vision and are in one mind in Christ.
4. You must be dedicated to the things included in your vision or else you will get distracted by other things that seem good.
5. Continually seek God for fresh direction. Be ready to move on when He directs you to.
6. Remember that it is not your talent, looks, or anything else but the Spirit of God that draws men to Christ. The Spirit that dwells in you will use you and speak through you if you will humble yourself and submit to God's will.

6. *Abounding Grace Ministries,* 1447 Cushing Rd. Plainfield, NJ 07062. Ricky Del Rio, Director.

New York City is quite a challenge for any street ministry, but where sin abounds, there does grace much more abound. I first met Ricky and learned about his ministry at the National

Street Ministries Conference. I was impressed by the way God had been using his ministry to have a significant impact on New York City. Ricky left a prosperous business to go into ministry, and he has used much of his personal funds to establish it.

He and his workers take a large truck to various parts of the city to conduct street meetings. They have a P.A. system in the truck and they play music and preach out of it. They give out thousands of free T-shirts that say "Jesus Loves You New York." As people get saved, and quite a few do, a staff member personally goes with them to a local church, helping the new believer get established in that church. They have developed excellent relationships with a number of local churches through this. They are a very giving ministry, and they have learned the truth of Jesus' words, "Give and it will be given unto you; a good measure, pressed down, shaken together, and running over, will be put into your lap" (Luke 6:38).

Abounding Grace Ministries is now an outreach of Faith Fellowship Ministries World Outreach Center. In 1986, they planned their first week-long city outreach, which they called "Jesus Loves You — New York/New Jersey." They are also planning outreaches for 1986 and 1987 in several islands in the Caribbean and in Brazil.

7. Christin Action Ministries, Box 220, Willow Street, PA 17584. Denny Nissley, Director.

The day after he was saved, Denny started witnessing to his friends who were involved in drugs and alcohol. The first one he talked to said he had plenty of time. After he and his fiance were married they would settle down and get religious. That night, Denny went home and turned on the TV. On the news, he saw their car smashed into a bridge. Both were killed. As Denny cried, God spoke to him, "Denny, you were the last Jesus they ever saw." From that time, Denny decided to fulfill the great commission.

Denny attended Christ for the Nations Institute in Dallas. There he got involved witnessing to pimps, prostitutes, and professional hit men. As he saw some of these people come to know Jesus, he made a commitment to God to walk the streets of the world sharing God's love. First he went to Greeley, Colorado and witnessed to whoever would listen. Later he went to Tulsa and worked with Jonathan Gainsbrugh at Worldshakers for Christ. Then, he went back to Greeley and started Christ in Action Ministries. After two years there he turned over the ministry to some local brethren he had discipled there and moved to Pennsylvania to do the same thing. God has provided his financial support throughout this period without him begging for money.

Denny's vision is, first, to equip and motivate the church to get off their pews and witness for Jesus and, second, to have busloads of "Holy Ghost hit men" in every major outreach in America, to see a street ministry in every town in America, and then to reach out to the rest of the world. Currently, Christ in Action is involved in outreaches to the Mardi Gras in New Orleans, the Boston Marathon, Ft. Lauderdale, Florida at Spring Break, the Indianapolis 500, and several other major outreaches. They also print four million tracts a year.

"No matter how big your ministry gets," Denny believes, "you still have a responsibility both to the lost and to God to make sure you are getting out on the streets on a regular basis. No matter how busy you get, remember, you are still called to be a 'street preacher' and that, I feel, is one of the highest callings God can place on a man. *JESUS WAS A STREET PREACHER!*"

8. Teen Challenge, Box 8591, Capitol Heights, MD (near Washington, DC) 20743. Mike Zello, Director.

Mike first started street witnessing with Dave Wilkerson in 1958, when he was 17. Now he is director of Teen Challenge in Washington, DC. One of his activities involves mobilizing Christians to conduct street meetings in the worst neighborhoods of our nation's capital. Workers would go door-to-door, giving out food, gospel literature, and invitations to the next street meeting. Their outreach began with an all-night prayer meeting. Each worker was given a special responsibility in connection with the street meeting. They would either get a permit or get permission to set up a P.A. system. The street meeting would include music, preaching, and at night a Christian movie. Last summer, they conducted 16 street meetings. They have recently purchased a 21 acre site to house a church and school to train others to be effective soul winners in the inner city of Washington DC and the rest of the world.

9. *Evangelism for Jesus,* Box 1646, Ft. Bragg, CA 95437. Scott Crawford, Director.

I spoke about Scott Crawford in the chapter on the history of SOS Ministries. Scott is a true evangelist who is always looking for new, creative ways to reach people for Jesus. God has used him to help initiate several new evangelistic works, such as SOS Ministries and the International Street Ministries Association (ISMA).

Two weeks after Scott was saved in 1970, the Holy Spirit impressed on him to go into the highways and hedges and invite people to come to Jesus. He's been doing that ever since, traveling all over the United States witnessing for Jesus. In 1981, Scott formed Evangelism for Jesus, which has a threefold vision:

1. to find, encourage and train evangelists nationwide.
2. to evangelize small towns in Northern California by working with local churches to develop local outreaches and area-wide strategies.
3. to encourage and help organize city-wide outreaches in each of the sixty largest metropolitan areas of the U.S.

Asked about key things for operating an effective street ministry, Scott gave this advice:
1. Count the cost. Run the race to the end. Although there will be many victories along the way, the major battles are only won through consistency. "Let us not be weary in well doing; for in due season we will reap, if we faint not" (Gal.6:9).
2. Don't stop evangelizing to get trained. Education is not a substitute for experience in evangelism.
3. Don't take on the whole burden of God. Just do the part Jesus

has given you to do. Build a firm foundation by learning to do one thing at a time well. "You did not choose me, but I chose you, and ordained you, that you should go and bring forth fruit, and that your fruit should remain" (John 15:16).

4. Keep in balance by spending almost equal periods of time in these four areas: Prayer, Bible reading, Fellowship, and Witnessing. Don't neglect your family. In the end you can only go as fast as they go with you.

10. Illinois Youth and College Ministries, Assemblies of God, Box 225, Carlinville, IL 62626. Gary Grogan, Director.

Gary is the overseer of all the youth groups in Illinois for the Assemblies of God. He also has a real burden for seeing his young people get involved in evangelism and he organizes a week-long outreach in Chicago each summer. Gary won his first soul to Jesus when he was in tenth grade and knew then he wanted to do this the rest of his life. Below is a paper he wrote for his denomination's magazine:

A Key to Successful Youth Ministry

I believe that obedience to the Great Commission is a key to successful youth ministry. Any youth group involved in active evangelism will be richly blessed by God. It is my conviction that the Holy Spirit is speaking to the body about evangelism. I am convinced that the missing ingredient of most Assemblies of God youth ministry is *personal accountability for fulfilling the Great Commission.* Let me suggest some practical steps for youth leaders to develop outreach ministries in the local youth group:

1. Teach and preach evangelism on a regular basis. Have you ever taught a series on evangelism in your youth meetings or Sunday school class? Is it time to do it again? Do your young people have a skeleton outline memorized that you have taught them on how to lead a person to Christ?

2. Role modeling is your greatest tool of teaching. Have your young people ever seen you hand a tract to a person and share

Jesus with them? Youth learn in the lab better than in the lecture.

3. *Schedule witnessing* into your overall youth program. Not only should witnessing be done in the summer . . . but young people should be visiting backsliders, friends, prospects, etc. during the week on a regular basis.

4. *Read articles and books on evangelism.* Make them available to your young people.

5. *Resist temptation.* Resist the subtle temptation of Satan to "wait" until your troops are spiritually prepared to be soul winners. The fact is they probably will never be completely ready. But it is our job to teach them and lead them. We must provide opportunities for growth.

6. *Use the element of surprise.* Unannounced, load your group up and take them to a park, mall, grocery store, etc. to "blitz." Have plenty of tracts on hand. This is a great starter experience, and you will be surprised if you announce a soul winning course on the way back to the church how many will sign up!

7. *Make big challenges.* In your preaching challenge people to use some of their vacation to be part of a special outreach. If the Mormons can get students to postpone their career education for a year or so, why should we be so Mickey Mouse about recruiting people to be a part of special ministry projects?

8. *Conduct outdoor meetings.* Every youth leader should learn how to preach out-of-doors! Drama teams and music groups should be organized which can perform outside where the people are. Only groups with pure motives, willing to go anywhere at their *own expense,* will be the ones that experience the true ministry of evangelism.

9. *Pray to be used.* It's hard for me to witness. I am almost always scared. It is something I have had to work at, pray hard about, and practice. I want it to be a lifestyle. Pray every youth pastor gets under the burden of a true evangelist: Souls!

We cannot afford to debate about the best methods of evangelism. We must do our best at follow-up, but not use it as an excuse not to witness. We must be more concerned about seeing God's dream fulfilled than our own. This is successful youth ministry. Only then can we bring back the King!

21 _____

The Great Omission

Seven Excuses for not Preaching the Gospel

"And they all with one consent began to make excuse" (Luke 14:18).

Two thousand years ago, eleven dedicated followers of the Lord Jesus Christ turned their world upside down with the message of God's salvation. They and their converts faced horrible persecution, were imprisoned and thrown to lions, yet their faith spread throughout the world.

Today, there are millions of Christians throughout the world. Modern technology has given us the means of reaching multitudes for Jesus. Yet every year the percentage of the world's population which has heard the gospel *decreases*.

Here in the United States, a large percentage of the population claims to be born again. The Constitution protects the rights of Christians to preach unhindered. Christians in the United States have more wealth and leisure time than ever before in the history of the world. Yet multitudes in this country, including many of the children of these Christians, are turning from Jesus Christ to Eastern religions, the occult, drugs and alcohol, and sexual immorality of all kinds.

In the San Francisco Bay Area, tens of thousands of Christians are attracted to Christian events. At the same time, a mere handful of Christians are witnessing on the streets. Millions of unbelievers go on in their sins, many of whom never hear a Christian witness. The voices of the political radicals, Eastern cults, and homosexuals are heard loudly in the streets and in the media. At the same time, the voices of the Christians are scarcely noticed.

What has happened? For one thing, the early church believed that when Jesus said to go into all the world and preach His Word, He meant what He said. Today, with Satan's help, we have developed many sophisticated excuses not to preach the gospel. In this chapter, I want to examine some of these excuses in the light of God's Word.

1. "I don't know how to witness." The early church didn't have any witnessing classes, yet they turned the world upside down with the gospel. Jesus said, "You shall receive power, after the Holy Spirit has come upon you: and you shall be my witnesses" (Acts 1:8). All a person needs to preach is to know Jesus Christ and be filled with the Holy Spirit.

2. "I don't feel called to do evangelism. That is the work of the evangelist and pastor." The ministry of the evangelist is to prepare God's people to witness for Jesus. Evangelism is the responsibility of the entire church, not just a few people. "And he gave some to be . . . evangelists . . . . To prepare the saints to do the work of the ministry, for the building up of the body of Christ." Eph. 4:11-12.

3. "I'm too busy to do evangelism. My job, my family, and my church activities occupy all my time." We find time for what is important to us. If we offered you $1000 to come witnessing next Friday night, the chances are you would come, no matter how busy your schedule. Is it as important to you to see souls saved from eternal hell as to earn money?

Witnessing for Jesus can be an excellent family activity. It gives wives a chance to get involved in spiritual ministry. It gives children a chance to see the reality of spiritual warfare, the ugliness of sin, and to acquire boldness in being used by God to reach the lost. Often, families are divided by petty carnal disputes. Preaching the gospel gets our eyes on eternal things, the things that really matter, and can heal divisions and unify families. All told, it has many advantages over that most popular and time-consuming Christian activity: television.

4. *"I witness at my job and to my friends and family,"* or *"My life is a witness."* We should witness in our everyday life, and our life should be a testimony of Jesus Christ. But what about all the unsaved people who don't have friends, relatives, or co-workers who witness to them? As the good shepherd will leave the 99 sheep and go after the one who has gone astray, should we not actively seek after those who are lost, that they would be brought to Christ?

5. *"Discouragement from lack of results."* Noah preached God's Word for 100-600 years, yet only his household was saved. Jonah had no love in his heart for the people of Ninevah, but the entire city of over 120,000 repented at his warning of judgment. Our job is to be obedient to the Holy Spirit, and leave the results to God. "He who watches the wind will not sow and he who looks at the clouds will not reap . . . . In the morning sow your seed and in the evening do not withhold your hand: for you do not know which shall prosper, either the one or the other, or whether both of them will be good" (Eccl. 11:4,6).

6. *"Satan."* Did you ever notice while you are praying, that you suddenly remember something you need to do, or find yourself getting tired and distracted? Satan will do everything he can to keep us from prayer, because he knows the importance of prayer. Similarly, often when we decide to go witnessing, we will think of all kinds of reasons not to go, or something will come up that needs to be done, or we will feel sick. Satan does not want Christians to witness, and he will do everything in his power to distract us.

The best way to combat this is to set aside a regular time for witnessing, and give it the same priority you would give to your job. Are you sick enough, or is this distraction important enough, that you would stay home from work on account of it? Is the salvation of souls as important as earning money? If it isn't, then we will never get around to preaching the gospel.

7. *"Lack of burden for the lost and lack of vision of the importance of evangelism."* How do we get a burden for the lost? We need to pray for them. As we do, God will give us a burden to

reach them. Also, He will open their hearts to receive God's Word, and He will equip us to witness to them. If we have a great enough burden for the lost, we will not allow any obstacle to keep us from witnessing. We will not let fear keep us from speaking with someone about the condition of his soul and we will set aside time from the busiest schedule to witness.

The missionary C. T. Studd was challenged to an all-out dedication to Christ by an article written by an atheist:

"If firmly believed, as millions say they do, that the knowledge and practice of religion in this life influences destiny in another, then religion would mean to me everything . . . I would esteem one soul gained for heaven worth a life of suffering. Earthly consequences would never stay my hand, or seal my lips. Earth, its joys and its griefs, would occupy no moment of my thoughts. I would go forth to the world and preach to it in season and out of season, and my text would be, 'What shall it profit a man if he gain the whole world and lose his own soul.' ''

How can we expect the unbelieving world or even our own children to take the gospel seriously when we ourselves do not take it seriously? When we as Christians start crying out to God for the salvation of those around us and are willing to make any sacrifice to reach them with God's Word, we will see unbelievers repenting of their sins and calling on Jesus Christ to save them.

22 _____

What Will You Do?

"Of making many books there is no end, and much study wearies the body" (Eccl. 12:12).

"You shall receive power after the Holy Spirit has come upon you, and you shall be my witnesses . . . to the ends of the earth" (Acts 1:8).

The early Christians did not take evangelism classes or read books on evangelism. They knew Jesus, were filled with the Holy Spirit, and obeyed His Commission. If this book does not motivate you to action, it has failed in its purpose. Knowing how to do something is of no value unless we actually do it.

I realize that every Christian is not called to full-time ministry as a street evangelist. But I think it is time we be less concerned with what we aren't called to do and seek instead to do *everything we possibly can* to reach the lost for Jesus.

What can you do?

1. Witness. Seek out opportunities to witness to people — your friends, co-workers, the person sitting next to you on the bus or airplane, the restaurant waitress. Is there an evangelism ministry in your church or city? Go out with them. Try as many different kinds of witnessing as you can. Go to nursing homes, hospitals, prisons, juvenile halls, door-to-door, shopping centers and the streets. Each of us is unique and will find that God will lead us into different styles of evangelism and areas of ministry. As we dedicate ourselves to reaching people for Jesus in every possible way, God will show us what He wants us to do.

2. Encourage other Christians to witness. Invite others to witness with you. Give your friends a copy of this book or some other book on street witnessing. Share your witnessing experiences in church.

3. Support street ministries financially. American Christians are very generous with their giving. They give over a billion dollars each year to their church, foreign missions, radio and TV ministries and other giving. Much of this money goes to good causes, some is wasted, but practically none goes to street evangelism in the United States. Most street ministries exist on shoestring budgets and find it extremely difficult to obtain funds.

SOS Ministries, for example, has been functioning for seven years and is very well known by San Francisco area Christians. We have three full-time workers, each of whom receive between $65 and $110 per week in salary! We don't want big salaries, but we do want to be able to support more full-time workers to reach San Francisco and other cities for Jesus. Do what you can to help, and encourage your Christian friends to do likewise. You may want to speak to your pastor or church missions board about supporting street ministries.

4. Pray. Pray for laborers in the harvest! Pray for revival in the churches! Pray for ministries around the world! Pray as much as you can! Pray fervently!

23 _____

The Future of SOS Ministries

Over the past seven years, I have seen SOS Ministries grow into a ministry that is having a significant effect on San Francisco and is helping raise up street ministries around the country. I do not know what the Lord will do with us in the next seven years, if He tarries, but in this chapter I want to list some goals I have for the ministry. Right now, most of them seem impossible, but with God nothing is impossible."

1. *Full-time street workers.* I would like to see 100 full-time evangelistic workers in San Francisco. Every major area of this city needs an ongoing witness in it. We need workers to witness to and disciple new believers from every group of people in this city — businessmen, tourists, prostitutes, street people, alcoholics and drug addicts, people of various nationalities, college students, etc. Some workers could organize daily outdoor concerts in various parks around the city and a massive "San Francisco for Jesus" march and rally every year with tens of thousands of believers taking a stand for Christ.

2. *Discipleship houses and families to take in new believers.* Right now, we have one discipleship house for new believers who need to get into a Christian atmosphere to grow in Christ. That house is almost always full. We need *many* such houses. For example, there are several thousand teenage runaways and "throwaways" in San Francisco. Usually, they survive by prostituting, selling drugs, and stealing. Many of those we wit-

ness to tell us they want to get off the streets. Right now, we know of no good place for them to go. We need at least one house for boys and one house for girls, so we can get them off the streets immediately. We also need to establish a program to train Christians to take new believers into their homes and disciple them. Discipleship houses are expensive and good house leaders are hard to find. But there are thousands of Christian families which could take in many of these new believers.

3. A year-round evangelism training school. I would like to see a school established in San Francisco where Christians could come to be trained in evangelism so they could start ministries in their own communities. There are thousands of cities and towns with little or no street outreach.

4. A team of evangelism consultants for new street ministries. Once our students return to their communities, they will need help getting established. I would like to see a team of evangelism consultants raised up to travel around the country helping new ministries get started and teaching evangelism in local churches that want to start ministries.

Friends, we don't need to see our nation go to hell! Millions of young – and older – people are being destroyed by drugs, sexual perversion, Satan worship, Eastern religion, and secular humanism. Many of them won't come to church or watch Christian TV. We need to go to them with the gospel. Won't you help us?

Larry Rosenbaum
SOS Ministries
PO Box 27054
San Francisco, CA 94127
(415) 552-2300